EVA SPENCER

How to stop binge eating

The step-by-step guide on ending bingeing + weight loss tips

First edition

*This book was professionally typeset on Reedsy.
Find out more at reedsy.com*

Contents

Introduction

This book is for you if you have trouble managing your eating. If you've ever binge eaten, you're well aware of the power food has on your life. You're bombarded with food thoughts every second of the day. Any food advertisement, fast food place, supermarket, and gas station has the potential to cause insatiable hunger. It's exhausting to be surrounded by food all of the time. Food gives you feelings of joy, remorse, dread, and humiliation all at the same time. You can eat and eat and never appear to hit a point of satisfaction.

After that, you're concerned with gaining weight and chastise yourself for your lack of self-control. You have a sneaking suspicion that it is too late for you and that you will be plagued by BED for the remainder of your life.

I assure you that you will reclaim your life. You should put an end to your binge eating for good.

This book includes everything you need to know about binge eating. This book takes you through the process of treating Binge Eating Disorder (BED), step-by-step. It also contains material on other eating disorders as well as weight loss and healthier eating tips. Additionally, this book will instruct you on how to assist a friend or loved one in overcoming binge eating. This book will inform you of the signs and effects of BED, as well as the threats and repercussions to your health. It will explain the reasons for BED and have contact information for helplines.

Stop spinning in circles and getting nowhere. If you read and follow the instructions in this book, I guarantee that binge eating can become a thing of the past.

Here's what you need to do if you're unsure if this book is right for you.

In this book, I'll teach you how to stop binge eating without being on a diet.

1

All About Binge Eating Disorder

What is Binge Eating?

Binge eating is uncontrollable eating. Objective binge eating and subjective binge eating are the two forms of binge eating.

The 2 types of Binge eating are:

Objective binge eating

You're eating around 2,000 calories or more in under two hours and the whole experience feels like you're on autopilot.

Subjective binge eating

You're consuming an amount of food that you think is excessive but isn't objectively high. The sensation of being out of control has remained.

BED (Binge eating disorder):

Overeating regularly whilst feeling out of control and helpless to stop could mean that you are going through Binge Eating Disorder (BED). BED is a widespread eating disorder in where you eat a lot on a regular basis and feel helpless to prevent it. You may overeat to the point of discomfort, then be plagued by guilt, embarrassment, or depression, or you may punish yourself for your lack of self-control, or you may be concerned about the effects of compulsive eating on your body.

Binge eating disorder strikes in late adolescence years or early adulthood years, usually after a significant dietary change. You can eat even if you're not hungry during a binge and eat until you're fully satisfied. You might also binge to the point where you don't realise what you're eating or tasting which can have negative externalities.

For a short period of time, binge eating may provide relief from uncomfortable thoughts or feelings of stress, depression, or anxiety. But then reality sets in, and you're overwhelmed with regret and self-loathing. Binge eating frequently leads to weight gain and obesity, strengthening the binge eating cycle (Smith et al., n.d.). When you use food to deal with negative emotions about yourself and your appearance more often, the more likely you are to do it. It will soon turn into a very vicious loop or cycle of eating to feel better, then feeling worse, and lastly seeking relief from food.

Regardless of how helpless you feel about binge eating disorder, it's important to keep in mind that it can be treated. You can learn to break the binge eating loop, increase your emotional management, develop a healthier attitude towards food, and take back control over your eating and health.

Binge eating disorder has now become an accepted form of eating and feeding disorder (Kumari, 2020). It affects nearly 2% of the world's population and can lead to additional health problems linked to diets, such as high cholesterol and diabetes.

Feeding and eating disorders are classified as psychiatric disorders because they are not solely related to food. People usually develop them as a coping mechanism for a deeper issue or a psychological condition like anxiety or depression.

BED is a recognized psychological disorder that requires more than just-food. To resolve the condition, people with it would almost certainly require a care plan devised by a medical professional.

Binge eating disorder is a widespread psychological medical condition that now affects millions of people around the globe.

Even so, with the proper treatment plan and healthy lifestyle changes, it is possible to overcome it.

Your thoughts about binge eating disorder

If you have BED, you may experience the following symptoms (*Eating Problems*, 2017):

- Constantly eating
- Feeling like you are too shy for other people to find out how much food you eat.
- lonely and desolate
- extremely low, if not worthless
- dissatisfied with your appearance
- Anxious and stressed

Symptoms

You may face these symptoms if you have a binge eating disorder:

- Eating a large portion of food in one go. This is also known as bingeing
- eat without thinking about it, particularly when you're doing something else
- Frequently consumes unhealthy foods
- When you're stressed, annoyed, bored, or unhappy, eat for comfort.
- eat until you're sick or uncomfortably full
- Don't reveal how much you're eating
- When you try to diet, you always find it difficult
- Gaining weight
- Constantly sick
- Have trouble breathing
- You'll experience sugar highs and lows erupt of energy accompanied by exhaustion
- health issues such as acid reflux and irritable bowel syn-

drome develop (IBS)
- Obesity-related problems like type 2 diabetes, high blood pressure, and joint and muscle pain will grow.

What does it feel like to suffer from a binge eating disorder?

Patients suffering from BED experience periods in which they consume excessive quantities of food in a short span of time while not being hungry. Following an experience of BED, you may experience a strong feeling of embarrassment, guilt, or regret. Emotional stress is a common contributor to binge eating.

During a binge, a person may feel relieved but afterward, they may feel ashamed or lose control. People with BED frequently express extreme dissatisfaction and distress concerning their eating habits, body shape, and weight.

BED is defined as a pattern of uncontrollable eating of abnormally massive quantities of food in a short time. These events are accompanied by a sense of regret, embarrassment, and psychological distress.

BED and your body

Binge episodes on a regular basis can lead to weight gain, which can exacerbate health problems including diabetes and heart disease.

What Causes Binge Eating Disorder?

Although the precise cause of BED is unclear, Several factors are believed to be involved in the disorder's development.

These are the factors:

Cultural and social:

Social and cultural factors may raise the risk of binge eating, such as a history of sexual assault. Emotional eating can be caused by external expectations to be slim, which are also influenced by the media. People who receive negative remarks about their bodies or weight are more likely to develop binge eating disorders.

Biological:

Compulsive eating and food addiction may be linked to biological anomalies such as hormonal imbalances or genetic mutations.

Psychological:

Researchers have discovered a clear connection between depression and binge eating. Binge eating disorder can be caused by body dissatisfaction, low self-esteem, and difficulty dealing with emotions.

What causes BED?

Body size

Obesity affects nearly half of people with BED and 25–50 percent of patients seeking weight loss surgery meet the BED requirements.

Gender

In the United States, 3.6 percent of women and 2.0 percent of men experience BED at some point in their lives. It's possible that this is due to underlying biological factors.

Genetics

BED patients may have heightened sensitivity to dopamine, a brain chemical that causes feelings of reward and pleasure. There's still compelling proof that the disorder is passed down through the generations.

Changes in the brain

There are signs that people with BED may have structural changes in their brains that cause them to have a stronger reaction to food and less self-control.

Image of one's body

People who suffer from BED often have a negative perception of themselves. Body dissatisfaction, dieting, and overeating all play a role in the disorder's growth.

A binge diet is when you overeat

Binge eating is often reported as the first symptom of the disorder by those who are affected (Mandl, 2019, para. 9). Binge eating during infancy and adolescence is an example of this.

Emotional distress and Life's trials and tribulations

Abuse, death, being separated from a family member, or being in a car accident are all risk factors. Bullying based on weight in childhood may also play a role.

Your eating disorder may have started as a result of a stressful event or trauma in your life (*Eating Problems*, 2017).

Here are a few examples:

- Abuse can be physical, mental, or sexual.
- serious issues in the family
- a dear relative or friend has died
- Exams or bullying at school or at work are examples of pressures.
- Other psychological issues.

Almost 80% of people with BED have at least one other mental illness, such as phobias, depression, PTSD, bipolar disorder, anxiety, or substance abuse (Overeating: Symptoms, Causes, and Seeking Help, n.d.).

Stress, dieting, negative emotions about body weight or shape, food availability, or boredom can all trigger an episode of binge eating.

The exact cause of BED is unknown. As for most eating disorders, the occurrence of this eating disorder is related to a number of hereditary, climate, social, and cognitive threats.

At what age do you get BED?

Eating disorders often emerge at the same time as major life transitions, such as:

- beginning puberty
- transferring to a new school or university
- beginning a new job
- attempting to understand your sexuality
- Leaving your house or relocating to a new location.

Family Issues:

Your family's experiences can either cause or exacerbate eating disorders. They could be related to specific childhood problems.

You may have managed to regain influence on your life by eating. Consider the following scenario:

- Your parents were especially strict with you.
- Your house didn't feel safe or secure to you.
- Your parents have high expectations of you.

As a product of your childhood, you might have acquired characteristics like precision and self-criticism. You'll be at risk for eating disorders if you have these characteristics.

Someone else in your family may have tried to lose weight, binge eat, or suffer from an eating disorder and this will affect you.

Social Pressure:

Eating disorders are unlikely to be caused by social or cultural pressures. They should, however, contribute to them and assist in their continuation.

We are continually flooded with messages about body image through films, magazines, social media, and advertisements. This can give us unrealistic expectations of how we should appear.

You may be comparing yourself to unrealistic pictures without even realising it (*Eating Problems*, 2017). As a result, social pressure like this could:

- cause you to believe you are not sufficient or good enough
- have a bad impact on your sense of self-worth and body

image

Eating disorders and social media

It can be difficult to avoid images of 'perfection' if you are using social media. Avoid comparing yourself or others to these pictures.

Be aware that many people use the following tools before uploading images to the internet:

- They may use apps that allow them to change parts of their face or body (*Eating Problems*, 2017).
- Filters that show skin that seems to be perfect
- To improve their overall appearance, using different camera angles, lighting, and photo editing software.

Remind yourself that images on social media are often edited to make them appear better than they are. It can be difficult but turning off your phone for a while may be beneficial.

However, it is possible that social media can support you in having a positive recovery.

Factors in biology and genetics

According to research, your genes and biology may influence your chances of developing an eating disorder.

Hunger, appetite, and digestion are all regulated by brain chemicals. Some people with eating disorders have been discovered to have varying quantities of these.

- Serotonin, a brain chemical, can affect your mood and appetite (*Eating Problems*, 2017, p. 21). Some people have too much of it, while others have too little.
- Hunger and fullness are regulated by certain hormones. Certain people are more affected by these than others, making them more prone to binge eating or overeating.

Eating disorders during pregnancy

Perinatal refers to the period between becoming pregnant and giving birth, which may last up to a year. Some people report that their eating problems worsen during this time.

'At risk' moments or triggers

Some things, while not the cause of your eating disorder, may be able to make it last longer.

You may be going through recovery right now, or you may have had eating issues in the past. Try to be aware of certain factors that may cause eating problems to resurface (*Eating Problems*, 2017, p. 22). These moments are referred to as triggers or 'at risk' times by others.

Talking about food and dieting with friends, for example,

maybe triggering. It could be beneficial to recognize the factors in order to understand how to avoid them.

How to tell if there is an issue

You may be unsure whether your problem with food and eating is a problem because it seems to be a part of your daily life. You should seek assistance If your connection with food and eating is having a negative impact on you. It makes no difference how much you weigh or how your body feels.

Some people refuse to seek assistance because they believe their problem is minor. They may not feel 'ill enough' to have an eating disorder.

It's also possible to have eating problems while keeping them secret (*Eating Problems*, 2017, p. 6).

Overeating or BED?

Many people have a natural propensity to overeat. Overeating and binge eating must be distinguished because BED is separate from overeating and a medically diagnosed eating disorder, not only a symptom or occurrence.

BED is a recurrent event of eating considerably more in a small amount of time than many people would eat in comparable situations, with events characterized by a sense of loss of control.

Furthermore, men and women who struggle with binge eating

often feel disgusted, guilty, or embarrassed, and binge eats alone to hide their behaviour.

While regular overeating may occur in people without this disorder, people with BED have frequent episodes of bingeing without purging, which can cause emotional and physical distress.

Another kind of eating that some individuals associate with BED is emotional eating. Although some individuals with BED overeat in response to mental triggers, this is not the case for everyone.

Even though you notice yourself overeating to the point of bingeing on occasion, this does not mean you have a BED. It all comes down to how much you gorge, if you fly off the handle and become unable to stop eating, and how you feel after and during a binge.

You most likely do not have binge eating disorder if you sometimes overeat so it does not bother you. You can have BED if you hide eating habits and feel self-conscious before and after bingeing.

Review page

As an independent author with a small marketing budget, reviews are my likelihood on this platform. If you are enjoying this book so far, I'd really appreciate it if you'd left your honest feedback. You can do so by clicking the link below. I love hearing from my readers and I personally read every single review.

PLEASE LEAVE A REVIEW:

2

Side Effects

Why should I stop binge eating?

- You'll feel more at ease

    To maintain homeostasis, or equilibrium, the body releases stress hormones when you overeat. That's why, after a large meal, you might experience a rush of increased heart rate or sweat, followed by a "crash" that causes lethargy and irritability.

- You'll sleep easier as a result

It may take longer to fall asleep after you have overeat. And if you do fall asleep, you might find yourself waking up more often because you're thirsty or have acid re flux. People who binge eat excessively are more likely to develop chronic acid re flux, or GERD.

- Healthy pancreas

When you're overeating, you're probably consuming foods high in sugar and simple carbohydrates rather than vegetables and lean meats. Your pancreas goes into overdrive after you eat the big slice of chocolate cheesecake.

- You will know when you're full

Ghrelin is a hormone that boosts appetite and is released when it's time to eat. When you're finished, your body releases another hormone called leptin, which suppresses your appetite.

People who binge eat regularly have lower ghrelin levels and have trouble reacting to hormones in general, according to studies. Daily binge-eating makes it difficult for your body to decide if you're really hungry or satisfied.

- You'll be more happy

It's normal for your brain to release dopamine, the pleasure hormone, after you eat a good balanced meal. Binge eating high-fat, high-sugar foods, on the other hand, will cause the brain to release dangerously high amounts of dopamine.

This means that if you have a habit of eating a pint of ice cream every Friday night, it would take more and more ice cream to produce the same amount of dopamine and achieve the same degree of satisfaction over time.

Trying to stick to balanced servings will help you get more of the satisfying feeling without the negative side effects that come with overeating. Your body will be much better and stronger if you stop binge eating.

- It's less likely that you'll get ill

Overeating and binge eating causes the tissues to be traumatized. The high levels of glucose and insulin produced by your body after a binge will lower your immunity for up to 24 hours, making you more susceptible to catching the bug going around the office.

- Your mind remains in command

Overeating and binge eating causes the brain to shut down, believe it or not. A change in mental state is necessary for the body to even accept it. Similarly, binge eating is used to suppress self-awareness.

Binge Eating Disorder's Consequences

Binge eating can result in a slew of physical, mental, and social issues. You're more likely to have health issues, stress, insomnia, and suicidal thoughts than someone who doesn't have an eating disorder.

Potential side effects:

- Anxiety
- Depression
- Substance abuse
- Weight gain

Despite how bleak this sounds, many people will recover from binge eating disorder and reverse its harmful effects. The first move is to rethink your eating habits.

What are the health risks?

Obesity and weight growth, as well as illnesses like diabetes and heart disease, have all been attributed to BED. Sleep disruptions, chronic pain, mental health problems, and a poorer quality of life are some of the other health risks.

BED has been attributed to a slew of extreme physical, psychiatric, and social health risks.

Obesity affects up to half of people with BED. On the other hand, the disorder is a separate risk factor for weight gain and obesity. Because of the elevated calorie consumption during binge episodes, this is the case.

Obesity can increase:

- congestive heart failure
- Stroke
- Type 2 diabetes
- Cancer

However, some studies have shown that people with BED are at an even higher risk of having these health conditions than people with obesity who do not have BED.

Sleep disorders, chronic pain issues, asthma, and irritable bowel syndrome are among the other health hazards linked to BED. Fertility problems, pregnancy complications, and the growth of polycystic ovary syndrome in women have also been related to the condition.

People with BED, as opposed to people without the disorder, experience difficulties with social interactions, according to research.

In addition, as compared to people who do not have an eating disorder, people with BED have a higher incidence of hospitalization, outpatient treatment, and emergency room visits.

Despite the seriousness of these health risks, there are a variety of successful therapies for BED.

Short-term threats:

- Aches and pains in the joints and other areas of the body
- Difficulty falling asleep or staying asleep
- Blood pressure has increased
- When moving, there is physical pain
- Nausea, diarrhea, gas, bloating, and/or constipation are all symptoms of digestive distress
- Heartburn or acid re flux
- Depression and other forms of mood dysregulation
- Headaches that appear regularly
- Pre-diabetes is triggered by hypoglycaemia

Long-term risks

- Diabetes type 2
- Stroke and/or chronically elevated blood pressure
- High cholesterol and other lipid levels in the blood
- Gallstones or gallbladder disorder
- Several types of heart disease
- Cancers of various kinds

- Problems of menstruation/possible infertility
- Swelling, joint pain, and/or decreased movement
- Disc herniation
- Osteoarthritis/arthritis
- Gout
- Poor wound healing
- Hiatal hernia
- Gastro Esophageal Reflux Disease (GERD)
- Fatigue/other sleep difficulties
- Sleep apnea or other serious breathing difficulties

Health consequences of BED

The most frequent health problem related to BED is obesity. Two-thirds of people who are clinically obese have BED; people with BED are usually of moderate or higher-than-average weight. BED can affect people of any weight.

Side effects along with binge eating

Both psychological and physical issues may arise as a result of binge eating.

BED can lead to a number of complications, including:

- Medical conditions that are related to obesity. Joint complications, heart disease, type 2 diabetes, gastroesophageal reflux disease (GERD), and certain sleep-related breathing disorders are all medical conditions linked to obesity.

- Life is of poor quality.
- Obesity
- Issues functioning at work, in your personal life, or in social settings
- Social isolation

The following psychiatric conditions are often related to binge eating disorder:

Anxiety
    Bipolar disorder
    Depression
    Substance use disorders

Effects and causes

BED is brought about by a number of causes, including genes, emotions, and life experiences.

Factors of social and cultural risk

The pressure to be thin can exacerbate your feelings and fuel emotional eating. By using food to comfort, reject, or reward yourself, some people unintentionally set the stage for binge eating. Children who are frequently subjected to negative remarks about their bodies and weight, as well as those who have been sexually abused as children, are at risk.

Risk factors associated with the mind

There is a definitive link regarding binge eating and depression. Many binge eaters are depressed or have been depressed in the past; others may struggle with impulse control, emotion management, and expression. Binge eating can be exacerbated by low self-esteem, loneliness, and body dissatisfaction.

Risk factors that are biological

Biological abnormalities may induce binge eating. The hypothalamus (the part of the brain that regulates appetite) may, for example, not be transmitting accurate hunger and fullness signals. Food addiction appears to be caused by a genetic mutation discovered by researchers. Finally, evidence suggests that low serotonin levels in the brain play a role in compulsive eating.

3

Warning Signs & Symptoms of Binge Eating Disorder

Warning signs & symptoms of binge eating disorder

Physical warning signs & symptoms of binge eating disorder

- Weight variations, both up and down, are apparent.
- Stomach aches, cramps, and other stomach symptoms that aren't precise (constipation, acid reflux, etc.)
- Having trouble focusing

Binge eating and compulsive overeating have behavioral symptoms.

- Inability to stop or regulate how much you eat.

- Eating a large quantity of food in a limited amount of time.
- You keep eating even though you're full.
- Keeping food hidden or secretly stockpiled for later use.
- When you're with others, you eat normally, but when you're alone, you gorge.
- There are no set meal times and you eat constantly throughout the day.

Emotional signs and symptoms

- Anxiety or stress can only be relieved by food.
- Feeling self-conscious over how much food you're eating.
- Feeling numb while binge-watching—as if you're not there or on autopilot.
- You never feel fulfilled, regardless of how much food you consume.
- You may feel culpable, revolted, or low after overeating.
- Desperation to lose weight and change one's eating habits.

When do you see a doctor?

If you're having some of the symptoms of binge eating disorder, you should see a doctor right away. Binge-eating disorders can range in length from brief to chronic, and if left untreated, they can last for years.

Discuss your binge-eating symptoms and thoughts with your doctor or a Psychotherapist. Inform someone you trust about your condition if you're afraid to ask for help. A parent, loved one, instructor, or religious leader will assist you in taking the first steps toward effective binge-eating disorder treatment.

3 or more of the following signs must be present for a healthcare practitioner to diagnose BED:

1. The person who is repulsed and guilty of themselves
2. The person is consuming food until uncomfortably full
3. The person eating by themselves because of shame and embarrassment.
4. The person consuming a large amount of food without becoming hungry
5. The person eating at a much faster rate than usual

BMI (body mass index) and medical diagnosis

Your BMI should not be the only factor considered by your GP or hospital doctor during your evaluation.

Unfortunately, your weight will influence your eating disorder diagnosis and treatment. You may have a serious eating disorder without meeting the diagnostic criteria. This can be extremely aggravating.

However, an eating disorder diagnosis is not required in order to access medication for an eating disorder. The therapy for the condition that is more related to your eating disorder would normally be prescribed.

How to prevent BED

Although it may not be possible to avoid all forms of binge eating disorder, it is beneficial to initiate recovery as soon as signs appear and seek professional support. Your medical care provider will direct you to the appropriate resources. Furthermore, teaching and promoting healthier eating habits as well as realistic attitudes toward food and body image may aid in the prevention or worsening of eating disorders.

If you believe a friend or loved one has a binge eating problem, advise them to develop healthy habits and seek clinical support before things get worse. If you have a loved one who may be binge eating, you should:

- Encourage and reinforce a positive body image, regardless of size or form.
- Discuss any issues with your child's primary care provider or someone close to your loved one, who might be able to spot early signs of an eating disorder and help avoid it from turning into a problem.

4

How To End Binge Eating:

Top 10 ways to end binge eating:

- DO NOT SKIP MEALS

Skipping meals will increase the likelihood of overeating and trigger cravings. Aim for three meals and snacks each for every day, separated by no more than three hours.

Daily eating battles two unhealthy dieting habits: delaying eating, such as fasting or missing meals, and calorie restriction (such as under-eating).

By avoiding problematic ways of dieting, mitigating any urges to binge, and reducing the frequency of binge eating, eating consistently and flexibly would help you gain greater control over your eating. You'll also appreciate the constant energy you'll have during the day!

Stay Hydrated

A quick but successful way to relieve cravings and avoid overeating is to drink plenty of water during the day. Other research suggests that consuming more water will help with weight loss and metabolism.

The amount of water that each person can drink each day is influenced by a variety of factors. As a consequence, to stay hydrated, it's best to pay attention to your body and consume water when you're thirsty.

Drinking more water will help you stay fuller longer, which will help you consume less calories and avoid binge eating.

Sleep

Sleep deprivation can be related to binge eating because it affects your hunger and appetite.

A higher body weight has also been linked to sleeping less than 8 hours per night.

Get at least 8 hours of sleep each night to keep your appetite under control and reduce your risk of binge eating. Beginning the day with a healthy breakfast may prevent you from binge eating later.

Plus, eating the right foods will keep you satisfied during the day, reducing hunger and cravings. Meanwhile, a study of 48 people found that consuming fiber- and protein-rich oatmeal improved appetite regulation and promoted fullness.

STOP DIETING

It's normal to feel tempted to diet after a binge to make up for your overeating and get your health back on track. Dieting, on the other hand, almost always backfires. Food cravings and the temptation to overeat are caused by the starvation and hunger that comes with strict dieting.

Rather than dieting, concentrate on eating in moderation. Find foods that are healthy and that you like, and consume only until you are satisfied, not overstuffed. Avoid prohibiting or limiting those foods, since this would only increase your desire for them. Instead of saying, "I'll never eat pizza," say, "I will eat pizza on occasion."

Fasting or removing certain foods from your diet has been related to increased cravings and overeating in research. Instead of dieting or totally removing those foods, concentrate on consuming nutritious foods.

Focus on making lifestyle improvements rather than adopting diets that focus on removing whole food groups or dramatically lowering calorie consumption to lose weight quickly.

Consume more whole, unprocessed foods like fruits and restrict instead of banning your treat consumption. This will aid in the reduction of binge eating and the promotion of better health.

Exercise

According to research, including exercise in your daily routine will help you avoid binge eating.

Physical exercise such as walking, driving, swimming, biking, and athletics are only a few examples of stress-relieving for binge-eating behaviors. Exercising has been shown to minimize stress levels and the risk of binge eating.

Exercise can assist you in losing weight, enhancing your body image, reducing anxiety symptoms, and elevating your mood.

Choose healthier foods

Trying to remove unhealthy items from your fridge and replacing them with healthy options can enhance the quality of your diet and make binge eating more difficult. A diet rich in protein and healthy fats, as well as daily meals and whole grains, can help to satisfy hunger and provide essential nutrients.

Fiber

Since fiber takes a long time to travel through your digestive tract, you'll feel fuller for longer.

According to some studies, increasing fiber intake will minimize cravings, appetite, and food intake. Fruits and legumes are only some types of fiber-rich foods. Fiber keeps you fuller for longer, lowering your calorie intake and hunger.

Protein

Raising your protein intake will cause you to feel full and enable you to control your appetite.

Have at least one source of protein in each meal, such as meat, eggs, nuts, or seeds, and consume high-protein snacks when you're hungry to avoid cravings.

Protein consumption has been found to reduce calorie intake, improve sensations of fullness, and increase GLP-1 levels, a hormone that can aid in appetite suppression. It also helps with metabolism.

Mindfulness

Mindfulness is a technique that entails paying attention to your feelings and listening to your body. This approach can assist a person to learn to detect when they are no longer hungry, which can help them avoid overeating. The practice of mindfulness meditation was found to reduce the prevalence of binge eating and emotional eating.

Look for someone to chat to

When you're feeling tempted to binge, talking to a friend or peer might help you avoid overeating. Stress is considered to be reduced by having a strong social support system, which may help you avoid other coping behaviors like emotional eating.

Pick up the phone and contact a trustworthy relative or friend the next time you feel like binge eating. If you don't have anybody to talk to, there are free eating disorder helplines accessible.

Step-by-step guide on how to stop binge eating

Step 1:

Take a pause to examine and comprehend your actions.

It's difficult to recall specific details without continuous supervision. So keeping a diary is a perfect way to keep track of exactly what's going on before, while, and after a binge.

If you're serious about losing weight, you'll need to track your progress on a daily basis before you've taken control of your diet.

You will be able to recognize the specific factors that are affecting your binge eating behavior through monitoring. One of the most important things to change is to consider what happens before, during, and after a binge, so you can find out what you need to focus on to avoid binge eating.

If you don't track, you're going in blind, trying to find out what's triggering your binges later. This is obviously ineffective. Monitoring will prepare you for rapid and long-term transition.

Things to write in my diary/journal:

- Date and time of the day
- What you ate and what you drank that day
- Where you went that day
- If you saw it as a binge or not
- Any other details that could better enable your current eating habits, including how you were feeling or your energy levels at the moment.

Step 2:

DO NOT skip your meals:

Plan for three meals and three snacks a day, spaced no more than three hours apart.

Eating irregularly, such as missing meals, and calorie restriction, such as under-eating, are also unhealthy dieting habits that can be avoided through eating regularly.

These two dieting habits have been related to a number of negative health effects, including binge eating, psychological impairment, depressive symptoms, and anxiety symptoms, according to reports.

By avoiding problematic ways of dieting, mitigating any urges to binge, and reducing the frequency of binge eating, eating consistently and flexibly would help you gain greater control over your eating. You'll also enjoy the endless energy you'll have during the day.

Plan and note down when you'll eat your meals and snacks each night. Since the initial emphasis is on gaining momentum, consistency, and regularity, don't think about what to eat.

You may even choose to eat in response to signals from your body, such as thirst. Binge eaters' cues are often disrupted, making it impossible to distinguish between appetite and satiety.

These signals should gradually return once you've established a stable pattern of daily eating, making you much more able to follow an intuitive eating pattern.

Step 3:

Address your issues

Do you find it difficult to successfully deal with a bad situation? If that's the case, learning how to solve problems effectively may be a smart idea.

Note that binge eating is predictable: it typically occurs as a result of an all-or-nothing reaction to a food law breach, and our mood fluctuates and intensifies as a result.

Working through these difficult times in a healthy and effective manner can help to avoid these predictable binges.

Problems may seem daunting and insurmountable at times, but remember that you are not alone.

This will be a valuable step - by - step solution guide:

- Determine the issue: My husband and I are still arguing, and I'm left home alone and depressed all of the time.
- Consider the following options for resolving the issue: I might eat, watch TV, browse social media, or go for a stroll.
- Consider the following implications of each solution:

Eat: This isn't a smart idea because, in the past, I've overindulged in order to ease my frustration.

Take a walk: Taking a walk will keep me away from temptation while still helping me to let off steam.

Watch Television: There isn't much on TV right now, so I'll definitely get bored and feel compelled to eat instead.

Hop on Instagram to see if other people are having fun: I'm not in the best of moods right now, but seeing how other people are having fun would actually make things worse.

Step 4:

Meditation will help you accept your condition

Meditation can be a useful method for dealing with the unexpected stressors and anxieties that we face on a daily basis.

Meditation forces you to sit back, relax, and become more

aware of, understand, and tolerate your mind's inner workings.

In other words, it stops you from impulsively bingeing or engaging in some other self-destructive actions if something unpleasant happens or when things don't go as expected.

So, if you experience a sudden change in mood states, an intense sense of tension, or a blow to your self-esteem, consider meditating for a few minutes.

There are a number of excellent meditation applications available for anyone to download.

Perform this meditation exercise before or after you've worked through your negative feelings using problem-solving techniques.

This will keep you centered and, with enough practice, will help you stop bingeing.

Step 5

Address and try solve your food anxiety

The foods you're trying to avoid are binge-eating trigger foods that cause you a lot of pain and anxiety.

Gradual exposure to all of these foods and moderate reintroduction into your diet will help you overcome your fear of these foods and their ability to cause a binge.

Generate a checklist of all you aren't supposed to eat. Sort them from "most banned" to "least banned" in sequence. Reintroduce foods from the "least banned" list into your diet gradually.

Put a small handful of cereal in your daily breakfast smoothie if cereal is on your "least banned" food list and you're still hesitant to eat it. You'll gradually realize that eating cereal has no negative consequences. You'll have disproved your misguided idea that eating cereal makes you gain weight.

It's possible that your fear about that food will fade, and you'll be able to enjoy a more balanced diet and life. Continue doing so for the remaining foods until you are no longer nervous. They aren't going to be a binge-eating cause for long.

This is going to be a lengthy process. Don't expect it to be effective right away. However, when you progressively reintroduce foods, you will find that you have less anxiety.

Step 6

Take part in enjoyable activities

Let's shift our attention away from evaluating your self-worth solely on the basis of your weight and shape and instead consider other facets of your life.

Your need to diet can diminish and your binge eating episodes can stop if you can broaden the spectrum of self-evaluation by elevating the value of other life areas.

Consider things that make you happy, bring you joy, or pique your interest.

Here are some examples of fun activities you could try:

1. Joining a volleyball club
2. Joining a tennis club
3. Trying yoga lessons
4. Try taking dancing lessons
5. Building lego or puzzles

The aim of these activities is to add more meaning to your life, regardless of your weight or form.

You will finally realize what matters most in life if you devote enough time and attention to these activities. Your desire to maintain a healthy weight and shape will wane. If you try taking part in these activities or others similar to it, it would almost certainly have a beneficial effect on your eating habits.

How to stop eating late at night:

Some people catch themselves eating late at night, even though they aren't hungry.

Late-night eating allows you to consume more calories than you require, resulting in weight gain.

Here are a few suggestions for avoiding eating late at night or in the evening.

- <u>Establish a Routine</u>

Getting into a routine will help if you are overeating or you're not eating enough during the day.

Structured eating and sleeping schedules will help you spread out your food intake during the day, allowing you to have a decent night's sleep. When it comes to controlling your food consumption and weight, getting enough sleep is important.

Sleep deprivation and short sleep time have been related to increased calorie consumption and poor diet quality. Over time, sleep loss will raise the risk of obesity and associated diseases.

Set eating and sleeping times to help you differentiate between the two habits, particularly if you have a habit of eating in the middle of the night. Having a meal and sleep schedule will help you break unhealthy behavior patterns. This will benefit you if you don't have an appetite throughout the day or binge at night.

<u>Recognize The Triggers</u>

You might find it helpful to search for a particular sequence of events that normally sets off your eating habits, in addition to determining the overall cause of your overeating.

Food is consumed for many reasons. If you are not hungry but catch yourself eating late at night, think back on how you got there. Frequently, you'll learn that you're eating food to fulfill a desire that isn't hunger. Due to a lack of daytime appetite, night-time eating will cause your whole eating schedule to be delayed.

Keeping a "food and mood" log is an easy way to figure out what causes your night-time eating and what triggers it. Tracking your food and workout behaviors, as well as your emotions, will help you recognize trends and break any harmful behavior loops.

Breaking the cycle of emotional eating requires tracking your behavior patterns and identifying what causes you to eat late at night.

Determine the root of the problem

Some people eat the majority of their meals late at night or in the evening.

To break this habit, you must first determine the source of the problem.

Overly limited daytime food intake can contribute to ravenous hunger at night, resulting in night-time eating. It may even be a matter of boredom or routine.

However, certain eating disorders, such as binge eating disorder and night eating syndrome, have been attributed to night-time eating. These two diseases have different eating habits and attitudes, but they can also have negative health consequences.

People use food to cope with stressful emotions such as depression, resentment, or annoyance in both situations, and they often eat even though they are not hungry. Binge eaters eat a lot of food in a limited amount of time and sometimes feel out of balance.

Obesity, depression, and sleeping disorders have all been related to both conditions. Night-time eating may be triggered by boredom, hunger, BED, or night-time eating syndrome. Identifying the root cause will support you in taking the correct actions to solve the problem.

Create a Meal Plan

You might find that using a meal plan as part of your routine is beneficial.

Planning your meals and snacking on nutritious foods will help you avoid eating on the spur of the moment and making bad food choices. Having a meal schedule will also help you spread your meals out during the day, which will keep hunger at bay.

Meal and snack planning will help you keep track of your food consumption and avoid hunger.

Seek Emotional Assistance

You can seek clinical attention if you suspect you have night-time eating syndrome or binge eating disorder.

A specialist will assist you in determining the causes and developing a recovery strategy.

These services often employ cognitive behavioral therapy (CBT), which has been proven to be effective in the treatment of a number of eating disorders.

Creating an emotional support network would also assist you in dealing with negative feelings that might otherwise lead you to the refrigerator.

Finding clinical advice and counseling for certain people with eating disorders may be crucial to solving night-time eating problems.

Relax and unwind

People eat when they aren't hungry for a variety of reasons, including anxiety and stress. Using food to regulate your feelings, on the other hand, is a bad idea.

If you find that you eat when you're nervous or depressed, try to come up with a new way to relieve negative feelings and relax.

Studies have found that relaxation mechanisms can help with eating disorders like night-time eating syndrome and binge eating.

Relaxation techniques such as breathing exercises, meditation, hot baths, yoga, light exercise, or stretching may be beneficial.

Instead of eating, consider calming methods, gentle exercise, or stretching to alleviate tension and anxiety.

Eat a Balanced Diet During the Day

Overeating at night has been attributed to irregular eating habits, which are also classified as disordered eating.

Keeping the blood sugar steady can be as easy as eating at regular intervals during the day in accordance with "natural" eating habits.

It can also avoid feelings of ravenous appetite, exhaustion, irritability, or a perceived lack of food, all of which can contribute to binge eating.

You're more likely to make poor eating choices and go for high-fat, high-sugar junk snacks while you're hungry.

Regular meal times (three or more times a day) have been related to improved appetite control and weight loss in studies.

In general, consuming less than three times a day is thought to impair your ability to regulate your appetite and food choices.

However, it's crucial to remember that the findings in this area have been varied.

It's possible that the best eating frequency for managing appetite and the amount of food eaten varies from person to person.

Regular meals can help you control your cravings and food urges by keeping you from being too hungry.

Every meal should contain protein.

Different foods can affect your appetite in different ways.

If you eat because you're hungry, including protein in each meal can help you feel full.

It may also help you relax during the day, preventing you from becoming preoccupied with food and avoiding late-night snacking.

According to one study, consuming daily high-protein meals reduced cravings by 60% and decreased the need to eat late at night by 50%.

Protein has been shown to hold you fuller for longer periods of time. Incorporating protein into each meal will help to minimize cravings and late-night snacking.

Junk Food Out of the House

Delete high-fat, high-sugar junk food from your home if you are prone to consuming it late at night.

You are much less likely to consume unhealthy snacks if they are not readily available.

Instead, stock your refrigerator with nutritious foods that you enjoy. When you're starving, you're not going to look for fast food.

Fruits, nuts, plain yogurt, and cottage cheese are all good snack foods to have on hand if you get hungry.

These are really filling and won't cause you to overeat if you get ravenously hungry later in the evening.

Remove any unhealthy junk food from your home. If you do it this way, you can't eat it all night.

You Should Distract Yourself

If you're bored and can't stop thinking about food, find something else to do in the evening that you enjoy.

This will help to occupy your mind.

Avoiding mindless late-night snacking may be as simple as picking up a new hobby or arranging evening events.

Find different things to do in the evening to keep your mind occupied while you're eating and you're bored.

Getting back on track after an eating disorder

It can be difficult to live with eating disorders while still trying to recover. You must think about food and adjust to your changing body on a frequent basis. There are, however, ways to assist yourself in dealing with these difficulties.

Starting to think about recovery

For different people, rehabilitation means different things.

It's true that you won't have any more eating disorder-related emotions or behaviors.

Thoughts and behaviors will also exist, but they will be less common. They may also have a less significant effect on your life.

It's possible that your perceptions of your relationship with food, as well as your perspectives on recovery, will evolve over time.

You may have the following thoughts:

- That you aren't having any issues
- That your actions are actually beneficial to you
- That your eating disorder feels safe, comfortable, or even exciting
- Fearful of the changes that will occur as a result of recovery.

And when you're able to try, whatever healing feels like for you, it will take a long time. It's likely that instead of weeks or months, you'll have to think of years.

If you are experiencing any of the following symptoms, recovery can be frightening:

- Fear of gaining or losing weight
- Fearful of losing control
- That your eating disorder is such an important part of your life and identity that you don't know who you are if you don't have it

If you've tried and failed to recover before, or if you've relapsed, you may begin to believe that you're totally helpless. But, even though it takes a long time, it is possible to feel better.

Dealing with misunderstandings

Many people conclude that eating disorders only influence young women. This is incorrect. As a result, if you're older or identify as a man, it may be difficult to share your experiences.

It's crucial to remember that eating disorders will affect everyone.

You may also notice that your physical health changes at a different pace than your mental health. You may begin to feel worse as you begin to look healthier.

Others may believe you have recovered when you are still having difficulty.

It can be helpful to keep communicating about what you're experiencing with someone you know.

Dealing with the opinions of others

Not everyone can understand how you feel if you have an eating disorder. Some people may make comments about your body, weight, or how much or what you eat.

People may believe they are saying something positive in order to assist you. They may not realize, however, that hearing that can be difficult for you. Since different terms support or harm different people, this can be very difficult to deal with.

Attempting to convey your emotions to family and friends can be helpful. Describe how a more supportive or helpful response would be.

It's impossible to always prevent people from saying things that aren't helpful. It might be a good idea to consider how you will respond to the things that others may say.

Managing your weight gain

For some people, recovery does not imply gaining weight. However, for some people, this is extremely difficult to live with. These suggestions have proven to be effective for some people:

Make a list of the reasons why you want to get better and refer to it when things get tough.

Take all of your out-of-season clothing to a charity store or sell it online.

Purchase some new clothing in sizes that you are comfortable in.

Don't spend too much time staring in mirrors or examining

your body.

Avoid weighing yourself.

Make a list of all the positive physical changes you're seeing in your body.

Talk to other people – complain or share your concerns with someone who knows what you're going through.

Avoid making comparisons or spending too much time looking at people's photographs in magazines or on the internet. Remember that these images are often manipulated or photoshopped.

Hard times in the year

There are some seasons of the year that can bring up troubling thoughts and behaviors. Christmas and birthdays are two examples of occasions where food and eating with others are important.

- Discuss what you're experiencing and what you think would improve with somebody you trust.
- If at all possible, come up with new ways to celebrate.
- Consider what you can do to keep track of yourself when times get difficult.
- Recognize that you may feel out of control from time to time.
- Do not be tough on yourself, and don't set unrealistic targets.

Self-care for people with eating disorders

This practical self-care advice will help you better manage living with and recovering from an eating disorder.

Consult with people you can trust

For a variety of reasons, talking about eating disorders can be difficult. People close to you may find eating disorders difficult to comprehend, but they will also want to assist in any way they can.

Beat, an eating disorder charity, offers advice on how to speak to others about your eating disorder.

If you're having trouble speaking, try writing things down. As an example, writing a letter can assist you in organizing your thoughts.

Seek out the help of others

Eating disorders will leave you feeling embarrassed, alone, and misunderstood. Speaking with those that are going through similar scenarios can be immensely helpful.

You should find peer support online or in person. These organizations will help you find support groups for eating disorders:

- Beat

- Over-eaters Anonymous
- Student Minds
- Side by Side (Mind's online peer support community)

Recognize how to handle relapses

It's very common to revert to old ways of thinking and acting. Especially when you're feeling stressed.

Try to spot cases where your eating problems are more likely to resurface. Here are some examples:

- Whether you're gaining or losing weight
- When the shape of your body changes
- Attempting to lose weight
- Going on vacation
- When you're pregnant and after you've given birth
- Exams, important events, going through a break-up, or moving house are all stressful times.

Consider your warning signs. Learn as much as you can about what you can do to keep things from getting worse. The following are possible early warning signs of a relapse (Remember it's okay to feel this way!):

- Feeling guilty after eating
- Suicidal thoughts

- If you feel "fat" and people around you are saying the opposite or otherwise
- Always thinking about food and weight
- Examining your body more
- Increasing the need to exercise more often
- Feeling hopelessness
- Feeling an increase in sadness
- Thinking more that you can only be happy if you are slim
- Feeling compelled to withdraw from those around you
- Feelings of needing to get away from issues and stress
- The desire to have more control over a variety of things is growing
- More weighing and evaluating if today would be a good or terrible day based on the results of the scale
- Choosing to skip meals or purging them
- Perfectionism thought reappears or grows in strength
- Avoiding food and/or food-related get-togethers
- Lying with treatment coordinators and/or family members
- Increased idea that if you aren't on a "diet," you are out of control

The majority of people will experience setbacks during their recovery. However, after each setback, you may discover that you have gained a better understanding of yourself and your eating disorder.

It's important to practice self-kindness. Accept relapses as a normal part of the lengthy yet manageable journey of improvement.

Change your bad habits

Routines involving meals and eating can be difficult to break. However, you may find that making minor adjustments will help. Consider the following scenarios:

- If you're concerned about overeating, buy smaller portions of food.
- When you find yourself concentrating on your body and weight, try to divert your attention. It may be beneficial to try a new hobby or interest that requires a lot of focus.
- If you're concerned about purging, find fun things to do after meals to keep yourself occupied.
- Consider some positive objectives that aren't related to food or calories.

Be cautious when using the internet

If you have an eating disorder, you will realize that you spend plenty of time, even without knowing it, analyzing your body to the bodies of others. We are frequently surrounded by images and pictures, especially on social media.

- Depending on how you feel when you're online, make reasonable adjustments to the sites you visit and the people you follow. It's fine to step away from social media or change your lifestyle so that it has less of an impact on how you spend your time.
- Keep in mind that many photographs have been altered to

make the subject appear different. It's possible that images on social media have been filtered or photo-shopped.

- Consider how you handle photographs of yourself. Do they make you feel bad, or do you feel compelled to alter them in order to conceal your true appearance?
- Consider whether you're following anyone whose photos make you feel bad or cause you to have negative thoughts. If you can, unfollow them.
- Any websites that promote eating disorders should be blocked or avoided.
- Look for positive eating and body positivity groups.

How to recover

Tip 1:

First and foremost, build a healthy relationship with food to help you recover from binge eating.

Recovery from any addiction is difficult, but binge eating and food addiction can be particularly difficult. Unlike other addictions, the "drug" is needed for survival, so there is no way to stop or replace it. Instead, you can cultivate a healthier relationship with food, one focused on satisfying your nutritional rather than emotional needs. You must do the following to break the binge eating cycle:

- It's not about avoiding fat. Dietary fat, contrary to common opinion, will actually help you stop overeating and gaining weight. To keep you feeling relaxed and whole, include healthy fat in each meal.

- Trying to stay away from temptation. If you carry fast food, desserts, and unhealthy treats around the house, you're far more likely to overeat. Clear the fridge and cupboards of your favorite binge foods to prevent temptation.
- Fighting boredom is a daunting challenge. Distract yourself instead of snacking while you're bored. Take a stroll, talk to a friend, read a book, or start a new hobby like painting or gardening.
- Giving care to the physical body. Understand the distinctions between physical and mental hunger. You're obviously not starving if you haven't eaten in a while and your stomach isn't grumbling. Allow time for the craving to subside.
- Concentrating on the food you're consuming. How many times have you binged in a trance-like state, oblivious to what you're eating? Be a conscientious eater rather than a mindless eater. Take the time to admire all those textures and flavors. You'll not only eat less, but you'll also enjoy it more.
- Eating on a regular basis. Don't put it off until you're hungry. This will just result in overeating! Missing meals will lead to binge eating later in the day, so stick to your mealtime routine.

Tip 2:

Find new ways to feed your emotions.

One of the most common causes of binge eating is an effort to cope with negative emotions such as stress, depression, isolation, terror, and anxiety. When you're having a bad day, food may appear to be your only friend. Binge eating can make emotions like stress, sadness, fear, depression, and boredom vanish for a short time. However, the relief is only temporary.

With the help of a diet and mood diary, you can figure out what your triggers are.

Keeping a food and mood diary is one of the best ways to figure out what's causing your binge eating. Take a moment every time you overeat or feel obligated to reach for your Kryptonite comfort food to find out what caused the urge. You'll almost always discover an unsettling experience that triggered the binge if you go back far enough.

Note down whatever you ate or wanted to eat in your food and mood journal: what you ate or wanted to eat, what bothered you, how you felt before you ate, how you felt after your meal, and how you felt later. You'll notice a pattern emerge over time.

Learn to accept and tolerate the emotions that lead to binge eating

Instead of succumbing to the urge to binge, take a moment to pause and explore what's going on inside you.

Determine the emotion you're experiencing. Make an effort to put your feelings into words. Is it stress? Is it a source of shame? Is it possible to have little hope? Do you feel irritated?

Is there such a thing as being alone? Do you have any concerns? Is it emptiness, or is it another thing entirely?

Accept the current circumstances. Negative feelings are exacerbated by avoidance and resistance. Rather than judging yourself or what you're feeling, try to accept it.

Investigate it further. What part of your body do you sense the feeling in? What are the sorts of ideas that are running through your mind?

Maintain a safe distance. Recognize that your emotions do not define you. Emotions are impermanent, like clouds passing through the heavens. They have no bearing on your character.

At first, sitting with your feelings may be incredibly awkward. Perhaps it's not impossible. However, you'll know that you don't have to gorge when you battle the temptation. There are other options for coping. Even the most intolerable emotions are only temporary. They'll quickly flee if you don't fight them. You still have command. You have a say in how you respond to it.

Tip 3: Regain control of your cravings

The need to binge seems to strike without warning at times. And if you're in the grasp of an intense and uncontrollable desire, there is stuff you can do to support yourself to keep in charge.

Instead of fighting the urge, accept it and ride it out. This is referred to as "urge surfing." Consider the desire to binge as a cresting, breaking, and dissipating ocean wave. You'll find that if you let the impulse pass without battling, judging, or avoiding it, it will go away quicker than you expect.

Distract yourself from the situation

Going on a stroll, calling a pal, watching an amusing video on the internet, and so on are all good ways to hold your time. If you become interested in something else, the desire to binge will fade.

Make contact with others. Talk to a friend or relative if you have the need to binge. Communicating your challenges will make you feel better and help you stop bingeing.

Wait, delay, and more delay is the order of the day. Try to stop the temptation to binge, even though you're not sure you'll be able to. For one minute, try holding your breath.

If you are successful, Extend it to 5 minutes if possible. You might be able to postpone the binge if you wait long enough.

Tip 4: Make a conscious effort to live a healthy lifestyle

If you're physically strong, comfortable, and well rested, you'll be better able to navigate the curve balls that life will eventually throw your way. When you're tired and overwhelmed, even the tiniest hiccup can send you off the rails and straight to the refrigerator. Exercise, sleep, and other good lifestyle practices will help you resist binge eating while you're going through a tough time.

Make it a routine to exercise regularly. Physical exercise boosts your morale and stamina while still serving as a powerful stress reliever.

Exercise's natural mood-boosting effects will aid in the reduction of emotional eating.

Ensure you get enough sleep every night. Your body craves sugary snacks that offer an instant energy boost because you don't get enough sleep. The emergence of food addiction has been attributed to sleep deprivation. Sleep can help you regulate your appetite, reduce food cravings, and increase your mood.

Make friends with others. Don't undervalue the value of close friendships and social activities. You're more apt to succumb to binge eating causes if you don't have a good support net. Even if it isn't with a professional, talking helps.

Take care of your stress. Finding alternative ways to deal with stress and other overwhelming emotions without using food is one of the most important aspects of binge eating control. Meditating, using sensory relaxation techniques, and practicing basic breathing exercises are just a few examples.

What other options do I have except binge eating?

To overcome any addiction, particularly BED you must find ways to get through periods of temptation and find alternatives to unhealthy behavior.

When you're feeling compelled to binge, consider the following suggestions:

- Take a stroll. Simply use your body and walk for 15 minutes and give yourself a mental break.
- Create a list of what's troubling you and write about it. If you have the urge to binge, keep a journal nearby so you can write down your thoughts and feelings. Don't edit yourself; simply download everything from your head and heart to paper.
- Breath deeply as you count to six. Before exhaling, hold your breath for another 6 counts. Rep for a total of 10 minutes or 4–6 times.
- Stop binge eating by setting a timer for 15 minutes. Distract yourself by watching TV, music, knitting, blogging, or doing something that demands total focus. You would be able to stop the binge altogether if you defer it.
- Contact someone you can rely on. Call a trustworthy friend or family member to vent about what's troubling you.
- Construct a containment box. Make a list of your thoughts and put them in the box. Bring them to the next therapy appointment and don't remove them until then.
- Clean and floss your teeth no less than twice a day. Taking care of your oral hygiene, as basic as it might seem, will help alleviate the oral fixation that is so often a part of bingeing.
- Make a list of at least five ways that bingeing is harmful

to your health. Be descriptive and provide both physical and emotional effects. A clear list will help you combat any justifications you may be making for why bingeing is acceptable.

- You may express yourself through art. Feel free to draw or paint how you're feeling. Make an attempt to be as articulate as possible. You may want to carry your work to your next therapy appointment.
- Complete a specific mission. Reorganize drawers or a wardrobe or balance your checkbook. Anything that helps you to refocus your energy and do something productive.

Exercise easy

Those suffering from BED tend to exercise in the same way that they eat, succumbing to an all-or-nothing mentality. This includes a limitation/binge cycle with food, and this all-or-nothing pattern with exercise typically shows as a period of no pain/no benefit exercise followed by sedentary behavior.

Because of the approach, rather than a lack of willpower on the part of the person, the no pain/no gain approach invariably produces psychological resistance to movement.

When you factor in childhood traumas associated with exercise (think gym class) and/or orthopaedic disorders and mobility issues that make movement painful, exercise can quickly become the "enemy" – something to be endured rather than appreciated.

Exercise Isn't So Dreadful After All
_____

Whether this attitude toward exercise stems from early experiences, recent experiences, or both, the end result is that it is avoided rather than accepted. Finding a way to move healthfully in the body will be critical for the BED recovery process in order to heal one's relationship with the body.

This change in perspective is what allows people to walk away feeling empowered and motivated to keep moving on their own. With that in mind, here are four key strategies for those suffering from BED to break free from the all-or-nothing approach to exercise and establish a regular routine of healthy movement.

- You must first center yourself

To do this people must reconnect their minds and bodies built on the practice of mindfulness. BED patients frequently feel cut off from their bodies, and the mission is to help them break free from autopilot mode and tune into their minds, feelings, and bodies.

Before beginning an exercise, this process necessitates the practice of centering – taking a moment to relate to your physical core and the here-and-now experience. This entails consciously aligning your spine so that, whether walking, strength training, or stretching, a person begins by actively tuning into their body before moving.

65

• It's easy

Training at a mild intensity (5–7 on a scale of 1–10) provides the impression that exercise is achievable, encouraging you to enhance your fitness without gasping for air or forcing yourself beyond your comfort zone. This method creates a psychological incentive for exercise compliance.

• Adapting exercise to one's current body

Learning to listen to your body's cues in the moment is essential for developing body awareness, reducing discomfort, and increasing enjoyment of movement, all of which contribute to increased exercise consistency and duration.

• Patience is required

The default button around exercise should be set to 'sedentary' before you begin, so easing into rather than jumping into an exercise program takes caution and patience to build on one's achievements. It is critical to keep one's expectations in check and then re-evaluate them on a regular basis in order to avoid relapsing into an all-or-nothing movement pattern.

Focusing on success metrics other than weight loss (e.g., increased stamina, strength, and flexibility) allows one to focus on self-care rather than measuring success through the lens of weight loss.

Discover the pleasures of exercise. It's important to try a number of different exercises to see which ones are fun – or at the very least tolerable – for you when it comes to exercise:

- Dancing is a fun activity
- Taking a walk
- Canoeing is a popular sport
- Snowshoeing is a popular winter sport
- Yoga is a type of exercise that promotes relaxation
- Pilates is a kind of exercise that reduces feelings of anxiety and encourages relaxation through the body
- Is it better to exercise alone or in a group?
- Using machines vs. going outside to exercise

Review page

As an independent author with a small marketing budget, reviews are my likelihood on this platform. If you are enjoying this book so far, I'd really appreciate it if you'd left your honest feedback. You can do so by clicking the link below. I love hearing from my readers and I personally read every single review.

PLEASE LEAVE A REVIEW:

5

Different Treatments

Why treatment

Treatment will assist you in developing healthy, balanced eating habits. It will also help you face and deal with the root issues that are behind your eating disorder.

Consultation with your doctor

It can be frightening to talk about your eating issues. However, speaking with your primary care physician or a hospital doctor is usually the first step in obtaining treatment. After that, they should be able to refer you to a specialist.

Self-help programs available online

In some cases, you may be able to get help from an online self-help program at first.

This may be the first option offered to you if:

- You're given a bulimia diagnosis
- You're given a binge eating disorder diagnosis
- Your eating disorder's symptoms are similar to either of the examples above.

Along with the program, you can receive brief support sessions. These can be completed in person or by a call.

If you're having trouble completing the program or finding it unhelpful, talk to your doctor about getting more help.

Treatments for eating disorders that include talking

You may be offered talking treatments for eating disorders, just as you might be for other mental health issues.

The best therapies which create healthcare best practices recommendations:

For eating disorders, Cognitive Behavioral Therapy (CBT) is used

This form of CBT is intended to assist individuals who are suffering from eating disorders. It may be used to cure anorexia, bulimia, or binge eating disorder.

- You should be given up to 40 sessions for anorexia. You should have sessions 2 times a week for the first 2/3 weeks.
- You should be given at least 20 sessions if you have bulimia.You will be given twice-weekly sessions initially.
- For binge eating disorder, group CBT sessions should be given first. If you prefer solo counseling or consider group therapy to be ineffective, tell your psychiatrist or doctor.

Therapy for the whole family

Working through problems with your family and with the help of a therapist is what family therapy entails. People with anorexia, particularly younger people, are often offered it.

You should look for scenarios that could be related to the underlying causes of your eating disorder. When you have an eating disorder, it will make the families accept and embrace you.

Getting access to talking therapies

Hospitals provide access to talking treatments. A referral should be possible through your primary care physician.

However, be aware that hospitals have long waiting lists. As a result, some people are considering private treatment. Appointments for private treatment must be paid for.

Among the possibilities are:

- You will locate a personal psychologist by a hospital or Counseling and Psychotherapy.

- Because of the cost, private treatment is not an option for everyone. You should try contacting organizations such as "Beat" for free counseling and support groups (the eating problems charity).

What treatments are available?

The course of care for BED is determined by the causes and nature of the eating disorder, as well as the patient's personal objectives.

Binge eating habits, being overweight, body image issues, mental health issues, or a mixture of these can be addressed.

Treatment methods include cognitive behavioral counseling, family psychotherapy, dialectical behavior therapy, weight loss therapy, and medicine. These may be accomplished on an individual basis, in a social setting, or as part of a self-help initiative.

Few patients only need one type of treatment, while others can need trial and error for different combinations before finding the right one for them.

A medical or mental health professional will help you choose a care plan that is right for you.

What treatments should I be given?

Cognitive Behavioral Therapy (CBT) is a talking therapy that seeks to help you cope positively with the underlying thoughts and emotions that trigger the condition by splitting things down into smaller pieces. It teaches you how to break negative habits and boost your mood.

- For binge eating disorder guided self-help is a good first move. This should include CBT-based self-help resources as well as supportive sessions during the program to ensure its efficacy.
- Community CBT is good for eating disorders if direct self-help isn't right for you.
- If group CBT isn't an option or you don't think it's right for you, providing individual CBT for eating disorders may be the best option for you.

These therapies are focused on what has been shown to be the most successful in the treatment of binge eating disorder. Please remember, though, that no two people are the same. If you don't think these therapies are working, tell the doctors who are in charge of your care. This isn't meant to be a criticism; rather, it's meant to provide them with facts that can help them work with you to find the care that is right for you.

Outpatient care can be used for the bulk of binge eating disorder treatment. When anyone is at risk of suicide or serious self-harm, inpatient care is normally needed.

Should I lose weight as part of my treatment?

As previously stated, weight loss should not be the primary goal of binge eating disorder care. Binge eating disorder may result in weight gain, but this is a symptom, not the disease itself. The aim of BED therapy is to decrease the occurrence of binges, fix binge-related emotions, increase mood, and boost metabolic health and weight in obese and diabetic patients. If you need to lose weight, you should make it a long-term plan to discuss with your doctor.

Although restrictive dieting may increase binge eating tendencies, maintaining a daily eating pattern is critical in the treatment of binge eating. Meal preparation and food diaries will be the subject of self-help advice and CBT-based therapies.

What medications are there to treat BED?

Several drugs for binge eating have been developed, and they are also less costly and quicker than conventional treatment.

Behavioral therapy, on the other hand, is more successful than current drugs in treating BED.

Antidepressants, antiepileptic medications like topiramate, and drugs used to treat hyperactivity disorders like lisdexamfetamine are among the therapies available.

According to research, drugs outperform a placebo in terms of preventing binge eating in the short term. Medication efficacy has been found to be 48.7%, while placebos have been found to be 28.5 percent effective.

They can also help with appetite, obsessions, compulsions, and depressive symptoms.

While these results seem to be promising, the majority of studies have only been performed for brief periods of time, so more research on long-term effects is required.

Headaches, stomach issues, sleep disturbances, high blood pressure, and anxiety are also possible side effects of medication.

Since many people with BED may have other mental health problems including anxiety or depression, they will need to take extra drugs to treat these as well.

In the short term, medications can help with binge eating. Long-term research, on the other hand, is needed. Medications aren't always as successful as behavioral treatments, and they come with risks.

Therapy treatment for BED:

The most successful way to handle BED is with clinical counseling and care from health professionals who specialize in the treatment of binge eating disorders, such as psychologists, nutritionists, and therapists.

The underlying problems associated with destructive eating behaviors will be discussed in such a treatment program, which will focus on the root of the problem.

It's important to focus on recovering from emotional causes

that could be triggering binge eating, as well as receiving adequate support in developing healthy coping strategies for stress, depression, anxiety, and other issues.

Furthermore, there are three types of therapy that may be hugely beneficial in the care of BED. These are the treatments:

- Dialectical Behavior Therapy is a form of therapy that educates people how to cope with stress and emotions.
- CBT (cognitive-behavioural therapy) is a type of therapy that seeks to help people understand how their feelings and impulses influence their behavior.
- Interpersonal Psychotherapy (IPT): Interpersonal Psychotherapy is a form of therapy that focuses on a person's relationships with family and friends, as well as how they see themselves.

In addition to these approaches, eating disorder support groups and group counseling sessions led by a certified eating disorder therapist can be helpful in establishing BED rehabilitation.

Why dieting is bad

Treating Binge Eating Disorder with a Non-Diet Approach (BED)

The significance of refusing to diet

It's only normal to be compelled to diet after a binge in order to make up for your overeating and keep your health back on track. Dieting, on the other hand, nearly always has the opposite effect. The deprivation and malnutrition that comes with strict dieting triggers food cravings and the temptation to overeat.

Instead of dieting, focus on eating in moderation. Find meals that are both tasty and enjoyable, and eat until you are full rather than overstuffed. Avoid banning or limiting certain foods, as this will only increase your desire for them. Instead of saying, "I can never eat ice cream," say, "I will occasionally eat ice cream."

Binge eating disorder, though not as well-known as Anorexia or Bulimia, is a serious condition that needs equal attention and clinical treatment in order to heal. The introduction of the 'Non-Diet' system is an important technique in dealing with BED. This technique teaches patients how to respond to physical hunger as well as how to control emotions related to food and eating. This approach, when combined with other validated therapies, will aid in the recovery from BED.

Binge eating disorder is described as having binge incidents at least twice a week for a span of six months, typically in the overweight population. Anorexia nervosa or bulimia are not present at the same time as the symptoms for BED.

BED is more common in women than in men, and it can lead to self-esteem problems for one's body, relationships with others, work, and positive feelings about oneself. In certain people, major depressive disorder, personality disorders, and substance-related disorders are all normal.

Many people who suffer from this type of disordered eating have tried a number of weight-loss strategies. Fad diets, pills, and the belief that they have tried anything except identifying their actions are examples of these. The non-diet approach emphasizes physical hunger over mouth hunger rather than weight loss as a goal. It focuses on improving self-esteem and body image rather than categorising foods as good or poor. A main aspect of the non-diet approach is learning how to focus on internal vs. external hunger signals and body discomfort. Being able to recognise that it is not consuming "poor" or (ineffective) foods that causes weight gain, but rather non-hunger eating.

Learning to concentrate on nutrition in reaction to physical hunger and normalising feelings about food are important aspects of this strategy as one progresses. Size acceptance is also something that one must identify with, as well as setting expectations that are achievable for their bone structure. Furthermore, since each approach is highly individualised, it is important to work with a Registered Dietitian, which is also known as an eating disorder specialist, who can adapt this approach to each person's lifestyle.

Orthodox weight-loss diet plans have not been effective in the long run due to mental conditions, according to long-term results. CBT, interpersonal psychotherapy, and antidepressant medications have been the more effective medication options. Long-term outcomes would be more positive if the non-diet approach is used in combination with treatment rather than the "fast fix" approach to temporary weight loss.

6

How to bounce back after an accidental binge

ow to bounce back after an accidental binge

H Now that you've eaten the entire slice of pizza or bar of chocolate or both, you might want to spend the rest of your days in a pair of sweatpants and think it is a reasonable life plan. They have a lot of room. So warm and inviting. It's really stretchy. And, best of all, they expertly conceal your body. Although a life in elastic pants may seem appealing at first, you may find yourself asking what to do after a binge after measuring the caloric damage of your food binge.

That's when the dream disappears and horror and terror take over. But don't worry: we're here to encourage you that it isn't as bad as it seems. The chances are in your favour that the transient weight gain and bloating caused by your binge will not become permanent features of your body.

Although it can take up to three days to feel normal again after binge eating, there are few fitness, food, and motivational ideas that may help you get back on track straight away. With the assistance of licensed dietitians, nutritionists, and physicians you can figure out the best ways to rebound from a binge and get back to your regular routine the next day.

Step 1: Forgive Yourself

It is not a crime to enjoy yourself. After all, you are just human. So, if you're overweight, bloated, and angry at yourself for eating too much, just stop. Dwelling on your binge would only make you feel worse, potentially leading to further mental bouts of overeating. The first step in getting healthy is to get over the shame. It's also important to note that if the overindulgence was limited to a single meal, the effects would be minimal. Normally, this would only set you back a day or two. Have your chin up and remember that you've got this.

Step 2: Hydrate

The final thing to do when you're done is drink water. It is, however, for your own good. Before going to bed, drink a huge bottle, and then a couple more the next morning. Holding a water bottle by your side for the next two days is also a good idea. This will assist in flushing out any extra salt that is causing you to feel bloated.

Step 3: Get sleep

One of the most effective ways to get back on track after a binge is to get seven to nine hours of sleep. What is the reason for this? It could make it easier the next day to say no to fat- and carb-laden trigger foods. People who were only able to sleep for 5 hours ate more the next day than those who were allowed to sleep for 9 hours, according to research. Researchers found that those who were well-rested had more "food discipline," while those who were sleep-deprived ate more calories overall, as well as calories from carbs and fat.

Step 4: Breakfast should be high in fibre and protein

It's the strangest thing: we swear we'll never eat again after a big meal, only to wake up the next morning feeling much more hungry than before. "What causes this to happen?" Insulin levels rise after a large meal. This is always accompanied by a decrease in blood sugar, which raises appetite the next morning. Rather than heading to the draw and filling your mouth with unhealthy cereal, make a nutritious breakfast with a mixture of lean protein, whole grains, and low-fat dairy. This will help in the digestion of the previous night's big meal and help you manage your ravenous appetite. Two eggs (or only the whites) paired with some avocado and a cup of fruit are a good example.

Step 5: Exercise

Seeing exercise as a way to counteract overeating is not a good way to think about exercise. This strategy can lead to feelings of guilt and remorse regarding one's eating habits. Furthermore, chasing every calorie with exercise is neither practical nor successful. Even then, working up a sweat the day after a binge can help bring oxygen to the digestive system, and will

81

make them feel better while allowing food to move more freely. Gentle workouts for thirty minutes, such as cycling, jogging, or viewing a fitness DVD at home. Make your ride to the mall into a mini-workout if you're low on time. From as far away as possible, power walk to and from the mall's entrance.

Step 6: Foods that are difficult to digest should be avoided

Keep away from stuff that could disturb your stomach if you're suffering from post-binge digestive pain. Gluten, dairy ingredients, coffee, and acidic foods such as fruit juice, pasta, and chocolate are also major contributors. Alkaline fruits, such as grapes and pears, on the other hand, would not upset those that suffer from acid reflux. Remove any known problem foods first, then see if there are any others you may need to miss for a day or two to rebalance.

Step 7: Maintain a 'clean' lunch and dinner

Don't go on a full-fledged detox after a binge. Eating "clean" whole foods the next day will help you feel better and in a good mood to improve your life. It is beneficial to prepare meals with a healthy combination of protein, fibre-rich carbohydrates, and fat. Here are some examples:

- Olive oil with some lemon dressing, 1 cup of quinoa and 3 cups of leafy greens.
- Baked chicken breast with 1/2 a sweet potato and 2 cups broccoli (steamed) along with 1 tablespoon of butter.
- Grilled steak, 1/4 cup avocado, 1/4 cup dried cranberries,

and balsamic vinegar on four cups of leafy greens and other vegetables

Step 8: Don't go hungry for self- punishment

If you're starving in between meals, eat something. Don't starve yourself just because you ate so much the day before. The day after a binge, missing daily meals or snacks would only fuel your drive to binge again. High-protein foods, such as two eggs with a piece of fruit, are recommended for promoting satiety.

Step 9: Allow for some wiggle room in your diet

Enable more versatility and independence in food decisions and meal plans during the week to reduce the temptation to binge. Classifying foods as "good" or "unhealthy" would only encourage restrictive eating habits, which will inevitably lead to binge eating when "evil" foods are reintroduced into the diet! If food intake and calories are regulated, there should be no foods which are forbidden.

Step 10: Reject the Scale

The day after a major binge, the scale is not your buddy. Owing to the extra food in your stomach and the water accumulation caused by consuming those salty pretzels, it may show a higher number than normal. Stepping on the scale after a binge can be demoralising and discouraging because it makes you feel like you've taken away all your success, which isn't always the case. Wait two days before measuring yourself to see how much harm has been done.

Step 11: Talk to someone

Like most challenges, the best way to overcome them is to confront them head-on and get to the root of the problem. Binge eating is a normal occurrence, but what caused it? Was it a case of depression or a quarrel with a lover? A quarrel with a pal? Or are you simply overwhelmed? It's better to get it off your shoulders ASAP, whatever the explanation. If you can't work it out with a friend or a parent, go see a therapist.

Step 12: Create an appointment with a dietician

Since binge eating is a true eating disorder—it's most prevalent in the United States—seeking help from a dietitian is the best hope for overcoming it. If anyone is having difficulty with this, they should not be forced to deal with it alone. Registered dietitians who specialise in eating disorders can help the person develop a positive relationship with food.

Step 13: Have your eyes out for the big picture

Getting one bad day out of every 365 days isn't so bad, after all! It is the responsibility as a dietician to not only inform clients about nutrition, but also to provide encouragement and teach them how to cultivate a resilient mentality so that they can bounce back quickly from a binge and stay on track toward their goals. Consistency is crucial, after all.

Step 14: Reframe Your Mood

The reframing strategy aids in shifting your viewpoint on the situation. Reframing is helpful because it affects a person's attitude in such a way that forgiveness is possible and the individual feels more in control of the situation. If I reframe my thought process after a binge, for example, it will change from feeling miserable to feeling like getting back on track. Your feelings are in charge of your behaviour. If we can ignore the bad associations that accompany binge eating, we are more likely to bounce back quickly from a binge.

Step 15: Eat more greens

Bringing back fresh fruits and vegetables into your diet is a sure-fire way to get back on track after a bad meal. Increasing your fibre intake by reintroducing healthy fruits and vegetables to your diet will make you feel more satiated and reduce cravings. Greens powders are a convenient way to get more greens on the go for those who choose to eat on the go. You can also throw in some chia seeds for added thickness and extra protein. Green tea powder and spinach is a fantastic choice that can be blended into any drink or added to a smoothie.

Step 16: Get rid of binge triggers in your kitchen

Are those cookies staring at you in your cabinet? Maybe you're unable to look away from the Costco-sized container of chips in the pantry. In any case, getting rid of trigger foods from your kitchen is a good way to prevent another binge. Any leftovers or snacks that could tempt you should be dumped or given away. Restock the pantry with nutritious foods.

Step 17: Start right now!

Note that each meal is a fresh start. Stop the attitude of "I'll start tomorrow." Start right now! Drink plenty of water, go for a stroll, and prepare your favourite nutritious breakfast, lunch, or dinner. Just because you're putting your life back on track doesn't mean you can't enjoy a treat now and then. You're simply resuming the safe routine that you want to be your way of life.

7

Healthy Eating

What I can replace unhealthy foods with

We understand how easy it is to eat too much and binge on sweets.
What's the harm in a chocolate bar here and a burger there?

Although there's nothing wrong with a little indulgence now and then, consuming unhealthy foods on a daily basis can lead to a slew of health problems, including heart disease, stroke, and type 2 diabetes.

According to the NHS, a man requires about 10,500kJ (2,500kcal) per day to sustain his weight in a stable, balanced diet. A woman's daily energy expenditure is about 8,400kJ (2,000kcal).

If carrot sticks and celery aren't your thing, here are some safe alternatives to some unhealthy foods. By substituting one for the other, you will continue to consume the same foods while still benefiting your wellbeing.

Dark Chocolate / Chocolate

You'll notice that consuming organic dark chocolate rather than milk or white chocolate is much healthier for you. Dark chocolate contains a lot of fibre and iron, both of which are beneficial for health. It's also high in antioxidants, which keep you looking young.

Sweet Potato Wedges / Chips

It's time to dump the chip shop chips in favour of something more nutritious and, dare we say, delicious. Sweet potatoes contain a lot of beta-carotene, which has been shown to boost blood levels of vitamin A. They're also rich in B6, C, and D vitamins. Vitamin B6 can help to lower the risk of heart attacks and degenerative diseases.

Frozen yoghurt/ice cream

Ice cream is simply churned fat and sugar that has been frozen. Frozen yoghurt includes probiotics, which help digestion and is lower in both. However, it is also very high in calories, and if you cover it in molten toffee, you exclude any health benefits. As a sweet and delicious dessert substitute, try mixing it with fresh fruit or nuts.

Wine, beer, or spirits

Here's a scary fact: drinking five pints of lager per week for a year equals 44,200kcal, or the equivalent of consuming 221 doughnuts. A pint of beer has around 180 calories when a single measure of spirits alone has 61 calories. When you combine that with some soda water and fresh lime juice, you've got a less fattening option. Also red wine, with 159 calories per glass and antioxidants, has less calories.

Chicken / Burgers

A typical burger can contain about 350 calories. A large 150g piece of grilled chicken breast, on the other hand, has just 220 calories.

Margarine / Butter

Although arguments about the health benefits of butter versus margarine mostly focus on the additives in margarine, using a good quality olive oil spread and baking with it will make your cupcakes light as air while also making them healthier. So use a healthy oil spread instead of margarine or butter.

Pizza pockets / pita pockets

Cheese layers, thick dough, and salty sausages are all delicious, but they're not very good. Why not make your own pita pockets instead of ordering pizza? Load warmed wholewheat pita bread with spicy chicken and salad for a balanced meal.

Popcorn / Crisps

Crisps are high in salt and saturated fat, and since they're usually eaten in a bag, it's difficult to know how much you're eating. Replace them with lightly salted or plain popcorn for a nutritious snack. To regulate the amount of salt you use, it's best to buy plain popcorn and cook it yourself. Popcorn also contains antioxidants, is rich in fibre, and is low in calories. Popcorn is high in polyphenols, which are antioxidants associated with improved blood circulation and digestive health, as well as a reduced risk of some cancers. Popcorn's high satiety is another health advantage.

Dried fruit / sweets

While we all have a sweet tooth, high-sugar sweets have very little nutritional value. Replace them with dried fruits that are healthier, such as mango, apple, or cherry. Dried goji berries, which are high in nutrients, are a super-healthy substitute.

Banana Bread / Cake

Most cakes aren't particularly nutritious, but if you want a healthier alternative, try whole wheat, organic banana bread. Whole wheat is high in fibre and potassium, magnesium, and zinc.

Healthy Eating Tips

Healthy eating is a crucial component of resolving binge eating disorder, also known as BED. Following these healthy eating tips can help you see food and eating as healthy and pleasurable instead of the unpleasant emotions that binge eating can bring.

- Start slowly and concentrate on making incremental adjustments for a healthy diet over time to set yourself up for success. Quick fixes have failed in the past and are doubtful to prosper.
- It's crucial to remember that it isn't only about what you eat, it's also about how you eat it. Slow down, chew deeply, and take pleasure in your meals. This is what mindfulness is all about. You should be able to enjoy your meals without being interrupted by a book, computer screen, television, or other interruptions. After that, your body doesn't even know or remember that you've eaten.
- Actually listen to your hunger and fullness cues from your body. It takes practice to learn how to judge your appetite and fullness, but you can start by observing how your body feels before, during, and after a meal. You'll be able to tell the difference between hunger and fullness after some practice, and you'll be able to estimate how much food you'll need to satisfy your hunger. If you're still hungry after a meal, wait 15 to 20 minutes and do something else to occupy your time. You will always be hungry after 20 minutes if you are genuinely hungry.
- Put a premium on variety. At - meal and snack, aim to include three or four separate food groups.

- To maintain a stable blood sugar level during the day, eat breakfast within an hour of waking up every day. Don't fool yourself into believing that missing breakfast would save you calories later. You'll set yourself up for later hunger if you don't eat a healthy breakfast.

- Healthy shopping precedes healthy eating. Make and stick to a grocery shopping list to ensure your kitchen is stocked with the right foods for you. When you're hungry, don't buy!
- Intend to cut down on trigger foods rather than eliminating them altogether. Cutting out those things completely will backfire, so eat them in moderation and tell yourself, "There's still plenty — this isn't the last time I can have this." "Enough is not enough."
- Consider what you should add to your meal plan rather than what you can exclude. The value of variety and moderation cannot be overstated.
- Pay attention to the foods and variations of foods that make you the happiest. Take note of the term "satiety." Satiety is a fun and grounded experience, whereas being stuffed is not.
- Keeping a food log is a smart idea. Food journals aren't just about people who have problems with food or binge eating. Journaling is a tool you can use to improve your overall healthy eating habits at any time and from anywhere.

8

Going To The Doctors

What to do if you're worried about going to the doctors about binge eating:

Visiting the doctor can be a terrifying experience. If you're worried, consider the following:

- Create a double appointment to prevent being rushed.
- Bringing someone you trust with you who can speak to the GP on your behalf if you're having problems, or chat about any changes in your actions or feelings that they might have encountered.
- Before you go to the appointment, write down any doubts, inquiries, symptoms you've had, and so on, so you're not caught off guard during the appointment.

Since medical doctors may not specialise in eating disorders, they do not fully comprehend binge eating disorders.

What if my primary care physician is unfamiliar with binge eating disorder or does not believe it is as severe as other eating disorders?

Binge eating disorder, like many other eating disorders, is a major mental illness and has to be treated right away. People with binge eating disorders need and deserve treatment. A simple, evidence-based treatment pathway for binge eating disorder is recommended.

"People with eating disorders should be assessed and treated as soon as possible." The earlier you receive treatment for your illness, the greater your odds of recovery are.

What if my doctor thinks anyone with an eating disorder should be thinner and be less heavy than me?

Note that your weight or any changes in it have no effect on whether or not you have an eating disorder; however, people with binge eating disorder can gain weight. Healthcare Providers should consider a number of indicators, including "an exceptionally low or high BMI or bodyweight for [the patient's] age." Please don't let this theory persuade you that you don't need treatment if you have an eating disorder. Don't let this fallacy persuade you that you wouldn't need therapy if you have an eating disorder. An eating disorder will affect people with any weight, and losing weight is obviously not a guarantee for people with eating disorders, so please don't let this myth tell you that you shouldn't need support.

Do not use single indicators such as BMI or length of illness to decide whether to get medication for an eating disorder. Such psychological and physical symptoms should also be considered.

What if my doctor is more concerned with weight loss than with the thoughts and feelings that underpin my illness?

A binge eating disorder is a mental condition in which you can gain weight as a symptom. Although it's possible that unrelated weight fluctuations contributed to the development of an eating disorder, it's highly doubtful that this was the only and direct cause. Focusing solely on weight loss does not resolve the underlying cause of the illness.

Weight loss is not the expected target of the treatments recommended to treat binge eating disorder. In reality, trained professionals advise that counselling includes recommending against attempting to lose weight during recovery by interventions such as dieting, as this can cause people to feel compelled to binge eat. Any eating disorder treatment should often discuss the root factors as well as the thoughts and emotions that lead to diet and eating problems.

Keep in mind that you have the right to receive high-quality treatment. If you're having trouble getting it, it's fine to inquire to see a different doctor. You can also dig into self-referral in your field.

Review page

As an independent author with a small marketing budget, reviews are my likelihood on this platform. If you are enjoying this book so far, I'd really appreciate it if you'd left your honest feedback. You can do so by clicking the link below. I love hearing from my readers and I personally read every single review.

PLEASE LEAVE A REVIEW:

9

Helping A Loved One

What would you do to help somebody who is suffering from BED?

It can be difficult for family and friends to spot warning signs because binge eaters frequently try to hide their symptoms and eat in secret. You can't always tell if someone is binge eating by their appearance. While some people are overweight or obese, some keep a healthy weight.

Empty food bags and wrappers, emptied cupboards and refrigerators, and hidden stashes of high-calorie or junk food are all red flags to watch for. If you think someone you love has BED, bring up your concerns. Starting such a sensitive conversation can be daunting, and the individual can deny bingeing or become angry and defensive as a result. However, there's a chance they'll appreciate the chance to share the struggle.

If the individual initially refuses you, don't give up; it can take some time for the person close to you to agree that they have an issue. Remember that no matter how upsetting it is to hear that someone you care for has an eating disorder, you can't make them adjust. They have to decide whether or not to try to get help. You can benefit by showing compassion, motivation, and support in the recovery process.

An individual with a binge-eating disorder can become an expert at concealing their actions, making it difficult for others to notice. Have an open and honest discussion with a loved one if you suspect they are suffering from a binge eating disorder.

Encourage and help your loved one. Offer to assist your loved one in locating and scheduling an appointment with a competent medical care provider or mental health professional. You might also volunteer to accompany them.

It can be difficult to love someone who suffers from binge eating disorder (BED), You want to be helpful, but getting too involved will backfire. These suggestions will assist you in finding ways to be involved without making them feel overwhelmed:

- Encourage them to seek support from a therapist. BED becomes more difficult to overcome the longer it goes untreated, so encourage your loved one to see a specialist as soon as possible.
- Be a helpful listener. Listen without passing judgement; this shows that you care. Remind your loved one that just because they binge on their way to rehabilitation doesn't

mean they can't improve.

- Be encouraging rather than reprimanding. Make it a point to only receive constructive feedback. Binge eaters already feel bad about themselves; using derogatory language just helps to sabotage rehabilitation attempts. You will make a meaningful contribution by being optimistic and expressing how much you care.

- Insults, seminars, and guilt trips should be avoided. In most situations, lecturing, being angry, or giving ultimatums to a binge eater only adds to the tension and makes the situation worse. State clearly that you worry for the binge eater's health and that you'll support them throughout their recovery.

- Lead by example. By eating well, exercising, and managing stress without food, you are incidentally helping your cherished one. Binge eaters, like all people with eating disorders, need positive role models. You will help them recover by becoming a safe person in both mind and body.

- Don't behave as if you're fully in charge of what they eat. Monitoring what someone eats is one thing that is well-intentioned but never beneficial. It just adds to the embarrassment and shame to be told what to eat, how much to eat, to be watched while eating, or to have food choices concealed, limited, or commented on. It adds critique rather than structure, which essentially repeats what the binge eater's mind is already thinking. Refrain from watching, commenting, or giving suggestions on what they're eating. You can share your love in a number of ways.

- Make sure you look after yourself. Know when to seek help from a counsellor or a health professional for yourself.

Helping others with BED can be overwhelming, but having your own support system in place can make it easier for you to assist your loved one.

- Don't place too much stress on losing weight. A popular question is, "How much weight did you lose?" Weight loss isn't the point of therapy, and your loved one may be afraid to come to you if they think weight loss is the only way to evaluate their performance.

- Don't put in more effort than the binge eater during their rehab. The binge eater in your life should be doing the majority of the work and speeding up the healing process. It's not that you shouldn't assist, but if you're doing all of the grocery shopping, keeping track of booking the appointments, or trying to persuade them to attend appointments, it's time to rethink your role. You probably mean well, but true binge eating rehabilitation necessitates the binge eater themself having a reason to step on and make progress.

What would you do to assist somebody who is battling with an eating problem?

Despite how helpless you may feel at times, you can do a lot to help.

You may have intense feelings if somebody you worry for has an eating problem. You might feel and think this:

- I'm really concerned about the individual.
- I'm not sure how I can go about asking them about it.
- Find it difficult to know how to respond to mood swings.
- Have attempted to assist them but discovered that they are unwilling or unable to accept assistance.

You may feel helpless, disappointed, and angry as a result of this.

The first steps toward assistance

At first, all you want to do is show the person that you care for them and that you value them.

Try to keep the following in mind:

- Let them know you're there for them . Verify that the individual knows you are here to listen and can assist them in receiving assistance. One of the really crucial things you could do is this. Tell them they can contact you whenever they're ready.
- Avoid becoming enraged or upset. They may already be remorseful for how their actions are affecting you. Make every attempt to be patient and understanding.
- Make no assumptions. Make no assumptions on what their eating disorder means before speaking with them. This may exacerbate their sense of helplessness. It may also make them less able to express and seek help for their difficult feelings.

Avoiding frequent assumptions

Many people believe that eating disorders are caused by certain behaviours or physical characteristics.

You may believe that:

- The major reason for eating disorders is body image problems.
- From looking at them, you can tell if they have eating issues.
- Only young women have eating disorders.

However, none of these claims are true.

Eating disorders can affect everyone. Persons of different ages, genders, sizes, and backgrounds are affected.

For people with eating disorders, coping with misconceptions is a daunting part of the experience.

Make no assumptions or judgments about the person you care about if you want to help them.

Developing the ability to comprehend their emotions

You may be having trouble comprehending the person's eating disorder. This can be extremely testing for somebody to accept how they are feeling or how they would feel as a result of your attitude or behaviour.

Consider the following scenario:

- Allow them to be patient with you. Keep in mind that their acceptance of the issue may take some time. Accepting it and seeking help will take a long time for them. They may not see their eating habits as a concern. They'd see that as a means of coping with those feelings. Rage, loss, helplessness, self-hatred, uselessness, shame are only a few examples. They may be frightened of what recovery will entail for them and their bodies.

Don't be too harsh on them. It's hard to convince anyone to change their ways. You may make a concerted effort to convince, trick, or force someone to eat more or less. This could make them even more anxious and afraid of food. It may also cause them to distance themselves from you. They may try harder to convince you that they are eating healthier, even though they aren't.

Don't get caught up in their appearance or make comments about it. Keep in mind that someone's weight or appearance has nothing to do with how they're feeling on the inside. When you say things like "you look amazing," you think you're being kind. However, for someone with an eating disorder, they can elicit extremely distressing emotions.

How you can help in a practical way

These practical ideas will help the person you're concerned about as well as improving your own understanding.

<u>You may want to try the following:</u>

- Take part in social gatherings with them. If they have trouble eating, plan activities that do not involve food. Take a stroll, watch a movie, or play a game.
- Make mealtimes as relaxing as possible. Don't make any remarks about their food choices. Allow them to eat whatever meal they are able to eat.
- Find safe ways to discuss it. Some people find that referring to their eating issues in the third person is helpful. "That's not you, that's the eating disorder speaking," for example.
- Assist them in locating reliable information and avoiding untrustworthy sources. This may imply looking for trustworthy information and online support. It also entails assisting them in avoiding websites that encourage unhealthy eating and exercise habits.
- Share other people's stories. Reading accounts and experiences from people who have eating disorders can be especially helpful for those who are willing to consider rehabilitation.
- Encourage them to seek assistance from a specialist. If they are hesitant to speak with their doctor, you might offer to accompany them.

Therapy for eating disorders in the family

If the person is a family member, you may be required to participate in family therapy as part of their treatment.

Working together as a family in family therapy entails:

Investigate what may have triggered the underlying feeling through deeper understanding of everyone's feelings and needs, seek options to advance together and support the individual.

Ask for a referral from your primary care physician or a hospital doctor to find a family therapist.

Even if family counselling isn't right for you (or isn't available), talking about your family's problems may be helpful.

Advice for your own health

It's critical that you look after your own health when helping a friend or family member. If you can, try to do the following:

- Keep in mind that recovery will take a long time. While their physical appearance may improve quickly, they may be experiencing emotional difficulties. Relapses are frequent, and they can be discouraging. Accepting this as part of the procedure will help. Don't blame them, yourself, or someone else.

Make an effort to approach yourself with kindness. It's difficult and exhausting to support someone who has an eating disorder. It's vital to note that your mental health is as crucial as your physical wellbeing, and you, too, are entitled to support.

Seek the help of specialised organisations. Dedicated support options may be available depending on your relationship with the person.

10

Other eating disorders

D espite the name's use of the term "eating disorder," eating disorders aren't only about food. They're complex mental health issues that often necessitate the intervention of psychiatric and clinical professionals in order to alter course.

In the United States, almost twenty million women and ten million men had or have had an eating disorder during their life.

Eating disorders are a type of psychological condition that leads to the development of inappropriate eating habits. They may start with a fascination with food, weight, or body type.

Eating disorders can have dangerous side effects if remain unattended, and can also result in death in rare circumstances.

Eating disorders may appear in many different ways. Extreme

dietary limits, food binges, or purging habits such as vomiting or over-exercising are seen in the majority of cases.

While eating disorders can impact people of any gender at any age, they are most frequent in teenagers and young women. Up to thirteen percent of teens could have had at least one eating disorder before the age of twenty.

Finally, eating disorders are mental illnesses marked by an obsession with diet or body image. They can affect anyone, but they are more common in young people.

What causes these eating disorders?

According to physicians, eating disorders can be exacerbated by a variety of factors.

One of them is genetics. According to twin and adoption studies about twins that were split at birth and adopted by various families, eating disorders can be hereditary. According to this kind of study, if one twin develops an eating disorder, the other has a fifty percent chance of having one as well.

Another factor to remember is personality characteristics. Neuroticism, precisionist, and hasty are 3 personality characteristics that have been attributed to an elevated chance of getting an eating disorder.

Possible causes include perceived aspirations to be slender, cultural demands for thinness, and exposure to advertising that encourages those ideals. In fact, many eating disorders are almost non-existent in cultures that have not been exposed to Western expectations of thinness.

Nonetheless, in many parts of the world, thinness is a culturally accepted ideal. However, only a tiny proportion of people in certain nations suffer from an eating disorder. As a result, a combination of causes is much more likely to be to blame.

Variations in brain structure and genetics, according to experts, can also lead to the emergence of eating disorders.

The brain's serotonin and dopamine levels, in particular, will play a role. However, more investigation is necessary before definitive conclusions can be made.

Finally, eating disorders can be caused by a variety of reasons. Among them are genetics, brain biology, personality traits, and cultural beliefs.

Anorexia nervosa

Anorexia nervosa normally manifests during puberty or early adulthood, and it affects more women than men.

People with anorexia consider themselves overweight even though they are dangerously underweight. They would rather keep a close watch on their weight, skip those ingredients, and cut their calorie consumption drastically.

The following are some of the most common signs of anorexia nervosa:

- When compared to people of similar age and height, being substantially underweight
- Eating habits that are extremely limited
- Despite being underweight, an overwhelming fear of gaining weight or repeated habits to prevent gaining weight
- A never-ending search for thinness and a failure to maintain a healthy weight
- Body weight or perceived body form has a major impact on self-esteem
- A skewed view of one's own body, including denial of being significantly underweight

Obsessive-compulsive disorder symptoms are well-known. Many people with anorexia, for example, are always thinking about food, and some may gather recipes or hoard food.

These individuals can often find it difficult to eat in public and have a clear desire to keep an eye on their surroundings, limiting their capacity to be spontaneous.

The two official subtypes of anorexia are restrictive anorexia and binge eating and purging anorexia. People with the restricting personality type will only lose weight by dieting, fasting, or exercising excessively.

People with the binge eating and purging personality style may consume a large amount of food or consume very little food. They detox after eating in all cases by vomiting, consuming laxatives or diuretics, or exercising excessively.

109

Anorexia is very dangerous to one's life. Bone thinning, infertility, brittle hair and nails, and the growth of a fine hair coating all over the body may all be symptoms of it. In severe cases, anorexia may result in heart, liver, or multi-organ dysfunction, as well as death.

Patients with anorexia nervosa may limit their food consumption or compensate by engaging in various purging activities. Even if they are extremely underweight, they are fearful of adding weight.

Anorexia talking treatments:

If you are diagnosed with anorexia, you may be offered extra talking therapies.

Maudsley Anorexia Nervosa Treatment for Adults (MANTRA)

This aids in your recovery by assisting you in understanding what keeps you bound to anorexia. You will gradually learn new coping mechanisms. This should be done at a pace that is comfortable for you and your requirements. At least 20 sessions should be presented to you.

Specialist Supportive Clinical Management (SSCM)

This isn't strictly a talking therapy, but it can be incorporated. You'll go to monthly appointments to get assistance with weight management, physical fitness, education, and counsel. You'll still get the chance to talk about any pressing issues you might have. It will help you understand your signs and behaviour better.

Focal Psychodynamic Therapy (FPT).

This treatment aims to assist you in comprehending how your eating habits relate to how you think and feel about yourself and others. This is usually only offered if other treatments have proven to be ineffective.

Anorexia nervosa

Anorexia nervosa is a condition in which If you've been diagnosed with anorexia (also known as anorexia nervosa), you're not eating enough. This indicates that you aren't getting enough energy to stay healthy.

Some people believe that anorexia is all about losing weight and dieting, but it's much more complicated than that. It's also linked to low self-esteem, a negative self-image, and feelings of extreme distress at its core.

Your emotions about anorexia nervosa

If you have anorexia nevosa, you may experience the following symptoms:

- I'm unable to think about anything but food.
- It's as if you have to be flawless or you'll never be good enough.
- It can be isolating, particularly if no one is aware of your

diagnosis.

- a desire for control, which you believe you lose when you eat
- that you're concealing information from your family and friends
- that you are overweight and afraid of gaining weight
- that losing weight is insufficient
- as if you want to vanish
- If someone questions your weight or food intake, you may become enraged.
- You're weary and uninterested in the things you usually enjoy.
- You may feel hopeless, depressed, or suicidal if you can't see a way out.
- Particularly around mealtimes, you may feel anxious or panicked.
- It's as if depriving yourself of food or over-exercising is a feat.

Your actions and anorexia

If you suffer from anorexia, you may:

- Reduce the amount of food you eat or completely stop eating.
- Count the calories in everything you eat for a long time.
- Food should be hidden or thrown away quietly.
- Avoid 'dangerous' foods, such as those high in calories or fat.

- Cook food for others without eating them yourself by reading recipe books.
- use medications that claim to help you lose weight or speed up your digestion
- Spend time pondering how to lose weight, testing and weighing yourself.
- Exercise frequently, adhering to strict guidelines as to how much you must do.
- Create a timetable for your meals.
- Make up food rules, such as listing 'good' and 'bad' kinds of food or only eating certain colours of food.

Your body and anorexia

If you're suffering from anorexia, you might:

- You should weigh less than you usually do or should for your age and height.
- lose weight quickly
- become underdeveloped physically, particularly if anorexia begins before puberty
- I'm really cold and tired.
- move at a slower pace than usual
- If you normally menstruate, you may have irregular periods or none at all.
- You may begin to lose your hair or your hair may become very thin.
- Lanugo is a fine fuzzy hair that develops on your arms and face.
- You may lose interest in sex or discover that you are unable

to have or enjoy sex.
- find it difficult to focus
- develop brittle bones or issues such as osteoporosis, a disease that causes your bones to break easily.

Bulimia nervosa

Another well-known eating disorder is bulimia nervosa.

Bulimia, like anorexia, seems to be more prevalent in men than in women and develops during puberty and early adulthood.

Bulimia patients often consume unusually large quantities of food in a short period of time.

Each binge eating episode normally lasts until the individual is fully satisfied. During a binge, the person typically feels unable to stop eating or regulate the amount of food consumed. Binges can occur with any form of food, but they are most common with foods that the person would usually avoid. Bulimia sufferers then purge to make up for the calories they've eaten and to alleviate stomach pain. Purging techniques include forced vomiting, fasting, laxatives, diuretics, enemas, and excessive activity. Symptoms can be somewhat close to those of anorexia nervosa's binge eating or purging subtypes. Bulimics, on the other hand, normally maintain a healthy weight rather than being underweight.

Bulimia is a condition in which a person If you're diagnosed with bulimia (also known as bulimia nervosa), you may go through a cycle of bingeing and purging.

Binge eating is when you consume a vast amount of food in one sitting. This is something you can do if you're having trouble dealing with emotions or problems in your life.

Purging is the process of getting rid of the food you've eaten after bingeing. You may feel guilty or embarrassed about what you've consumed.

Bulimia and how it affects your emotions

If you have bulimia, you may experience the following symptoms:

- shame and remorse
- hatred for your own body
- that you are overweight
- afraid of being discovered by family and friends
- anxious or depressed
- It can be isolating, particularly if no one is aware of your diagnosis.
- very depressed, sad, and angry
- mood swings that come on quickly or unexpectedly
- stuck in a cycle of feeling powerless and attempting to reclaim it
- numb, as if bingeing or purging has blocked out emotions.

Your actions and bulimia

If you suffer from bulimia, you may:

- consume a lots of food at once (binge)
- On a regular basis, I feed, feel guilty, purge, feel hungry, and eat again.
- binge on foods that you believe are bad for you.
- Between binges, starve yourself.
- eating in secret
- Only certain foods pique your interest.
- Make yourself ill, use laxatives, or exercise a lot to get rid of the food you've eaten (purge).

Bulimia and your body

When you have bulimia, you might:

- Maintain a constant weight or go through a lot of weight fluctuations
- be dehydrated, which may cause skin issues
- If you usually menstruate, you can have irregular or non-existent cycles.
- Stomach acid will hurt your teeth and cause a sore throat if you make yourself sick.
- You can experience irritable bowel syndrome (IBS), a stretched colon, constipation, or cardiac failure if you use laxatives.

The following are some of the most common bulimia nervosa symptoms:

- recurrent episodes of binge feeding accompanied by a sense of powerlessness
- recurrent episodes of indiscriminate purging to avoid weight gain
- A sense of self-worth that is heavily influenced by one's body type and weight
- a fear of adding weight while being of medium weight

A swollen and raw throat, swollen salivary glands, worn tooth enamel, tooth loss, acid reflux, gut inflammation, extreme dehydration, and hormonal disruptions are all possible bulimia side effects.

Bulimia can also induce an electrolyte imbalance, such as sodium, potassium, and calcium, in extreme cases. A stroke or heart attack may occur as a result of this.

Bulimia nervosa patients eat a lot of food in a short amount of time and then purge. Despite being at a good weight, they are afraid of adding weight.

Pica

Pica causes you to eat items that aren't food on a regular basis. The foods you consume are commonly nutritionally deficient. Such examples include chalk, metal, and paint. This can be very dangerous to your life. Pica is a form of eating disorder that involves the ingestion of non-food items.

Non-food products such as wool are highly desired by Pica patients. Pica can affect both adults and children and adolescents. The most common patients of this disease are children, pregnant ladies, and mentally ill people.

Food toxicity, infections, gut injury, and dietary deficits may be more common in Pica victims. Pica can be lethal depending on the substances consumed.

Pica, on the other hand, requires that consuming non-food substances is not a popular part of someone's culture or religion. Furthermore, it must not be regarded as a socially appropriate activity by one's peers.

Pica patients have a strong desire for and use of non-food substances. This condition is more likely to affect infants, pregnant women, and people with mental illnesses.

Rumination Disorder

You can regurgitate your meals on a daily basis if you have rumination disorder. Regurgitating is the process of returning food to the stomach after it has been eaten.

You won't be capable of putting it down to a physical issue. You can chew, swallow, or spit out the food you regurgitate.

Ruminative disorder is a newly defined eating disorder. It's a condition in which a human regurgitates previously chewed and swallowed food, re-chews it, and then swallows or spits it out. This ruminating usually occurs within the first 30 minutes of a meal. It's not a medical condition like reflux, and it's completely voluntary.

This condition may occur in infancy, adolescence, or adulthood. It typically occurs in children between the ages of 3 and 12 months and then goes away on its own. The disorder normally necessitates treatment for both children and adults.

If left untreated, rumination disorder in infants may lead to weight loss and extreme malnutrition, which can be fatal.

Adults with this condition should control their food consumption, particularly while they are out in public. As a consequence, it's likely that they'll lose weight and become underweight.

Anybody of any age may be affected by rumination disorder. The disease causes people to vomit out the food they just eat. They chew it some more before swallowing or vomiting it out.

Avoidant/restrictive food intake disorder (ARFID)

If you've been diagnosed with **Avoidant/restrictive food intake disorder (ARFID)**, you'll feel compelled to avoid some foods (or all foods). This may be due to a particular odour, flavour, or texture. It's possible that the thought of eating makes you feel anxious.

ARFID isn't usually associated with body image issues. It's more about the act of eating than anything else.

Avoidant/restrictive food eating disorder is a new term for a similar illness (ARFID).

The term "eating disorder of infancy and early childhood" has been replaced by "food disorder of infancy and early childhood," which was historically used to describe an illness that only affected children under the age of seven.

Though ARFID is most common in childhood and adolescence, it can also affect adults. Furthermore, it has an equitable impact on men and women.

Disturbed eating is a symptom of this condition, and it may be caused by a lack of appetite or a dislike for certain smells, tastes, colours, textures, or temperatures.

The following are some of the most common ARFID symptoms:

- Food avoidance or restriction that prevents a person from getting enough calories or nutrients
- Eating behaviours that make it difficult to engage in normal social activities, such as eating with others
- Loss of weight or a lack of growth for one's age and height
- nutrient shortages, supplement reliance, or tube feeding

It's important to remember that ARFID extends beyond common habits like toddler pickiness or older adults' reduced food intake.

Furthermore, it excludes food avoidance or restriction due to a lack of availability or religious or cultural traditions.

ARFID is an eating disorder in which people consume too little food. This may be attributed to a lack of interest in food or a strong hatred of the appearance, scent, or taste of such foods.

Purging disorder

Purging habits, such as vomiting, laxatives, diuretics, or excessive exercise, are often used by people with purging dysfunction to regulate their weight or form. They should not, though, binge.

Night eating syndrome

Night eating syndrome is a disorder in which a person who eats Individuals with this syndrome sometimes overeats, especially after waking up from a nap.

Other specified feeding or eating disorder (OSFED)

This category covers all such diseases with symptoms that are similar to those of an eating disorder but do not fit into any of the categories above and are not covered by the DSM-5.

Orthorexia is one of the diseases that can fall under OSFED.

Despite widespread television coverage and academic reports, the current DSM does not recognise orthorexia as a separate eating disorder.

Orthorexia is a condition that involves people who have an obsession with healthy eating to the extent where it disrupts their daily lives.

For example, the affected individual can remove entire food groups out of fear of becoming ill. Malnutrition, extreme weight loss, trouble eating outside the house, and emotional distress may all result from this.

Weight reduction is rarely a priority for people with orthorexia. Instead, how well they adhere to their self-imposed diet guidelines determines their self-worth, identity, and happiness.

You have an eating disorder if you receive an OSFED diagnosis. You, on the other hand, do not meet any of the anorexia, bulimia, or binge eating disorder criteria. This does not negate the severity of your eating disorder.

OSFED simply means that your condition does not fit into any of the current diagnoses. Receiving an OSFED diagnosis will assist you in receiving treatment and support. You may have any of the emotions, actions, or physical changes associated with other eating disorders. OSFED was previously known as "eating disorder not otherwise specified" (EDNOS).

Overall

Some eating disorders that aren't well understood include purging disease and night feeding syndrome. OSFED encompasses all eating disorders that do not fit into another grouping, such as orthorexia.

The headings above are meant to help you understand the most common eating disorders and debunk common myths around them. Eating disorders are common medical disorders that need treatment. They could be harmful to the body if not treated.

If you or someone you know has an eating problem, you should seek treatment from an eating disorder specialist.

Medication to treat eating disorders

Eating disorders are not treated with special medications. However, if you have underlying issues like depression or anxiety, you may be prescribed medication. For example, you may be prescribed an antidepressant to help you cope with your emotions.

You should be prescribed drugs in addition to counselling. Medication should not be the only option available to you. Your doctor will decide whether or not to prescribe drugs to you, and you will have the final say on whether or not to take it.

Drugs are absorbed more quickly into your bloodstream if you're underweight due to an eating disorder. This may make any drug more dangerous or ineffective than it needs to be.

Involvement in a hospital or clinic

Because of your eating disorder, you may need to visit a hospital or clinic. This may be required if:

- your doctor or health-care team thinks you're sick or underweight
- Other treatments haven't been successful.
- It's difficult for you to stay healthy in your home.

How long must I remain?

If you're an outpatient or day resident, you'll be able to go home most nights and weekends. You'll spend the rest of the time in the hospital or clinic whether you're an inpatient. The duration of your stay will be decided by how much help you need to get back on your feet.

What kind of assistance and therapy am I eligible for?

As an inpatient, you'll usually get a variety of services. The hospital or clinic's staff may include the following individuals:

- Doctors
- Dieticians
- psychotherapists
- occupational therapists
- social workers
- family and relationship therapists

- specialist nurses

The following treatments may be used:

- Therapies that include talking
- prescription drugs
- Refeeding
- working in groups of those who are dealing with eating disorders

Throughout your stay, your weight and general health will be monitored. You can also get assistance with:

- Purchasing, preparing, and serving meals are all tasks that must be completed.
- how to deal with fear and stress
- how to be more self-assured
- how to control anger and communicate effectively

What exactly is refeeding?

Refeeding is when you are given meals to help you get back to a healthy weight.

It entails assisting you in gaining weight in order to increase your energy levels and physical health. Certain meals may be offered to you because of their nutritional value. Or foods that are especially effective at aiding weight gain.

The process of refeeding differs from one clinic to the next. Some doctors can do this progressively over time to help you to gain weight. Others would like to see you get back to a healthier weight as quickly as possible.

This can be a challenging task, particularly if you want to stop gaining weight. You should talk to a primary care provider or a hospital doctor about it in more depth.

What if I don't live in close proximity to a clinic?

There are just a handful eating disorder clinics. As a consequence, getting counselling close to your home might not always be possible.

This may mean travelling to a certain clinic or going to a general mental health hospital.If you want to learn more about specialised clinics, talk to your doctor or your care team.

Private treatment centres are also available. Some may provide treatment similar to that provided by clinics. Others offer a larger selection of complementary and art therapies.

Is it possible that I'll be compelled to go to the hospital?

Under the Mental Health Act, you may be compelled to enter a mental health facility. This is commonly referred to as sectioning.' If your health or safety is in jeopardy, or to protect others, you may be sectioned.

Health professionals will examine you before sectioning you. You might be partitioned if you have an eating disorder, for example:

- It has a significant detrimental impact on your fitness and well-being.
- You will be unable to recover without medical help.
- It's likely that your mental health will suffer as a result of your actions.

If you have been sectioned, you may be treated against your will during your hospital stay. Refeeding, for example, may be used to treat an eating disorder without your consent.

Other issues with eating and feeding

You may be diagnosed with one of the eating disorders listed on this page as a result of your eating problem.

Other diagnoses, on the other hand, may be given to you.

Anorexia nervosa, bulimia nervosa, and binge eating disorder are also more popular.

Review page

As an independent author with a small marketing budget, reviews are my likelihood on this platform. If you are enjoying this book so far, I'd really appreciate it if you'd left your honest feedback. You can do so by clicking the link below. I love hearing from my readers and I personally read every single review.

PLEASE LEAVE A REVIEW:

11

Mental Health

Depression and BED

Depression is often related to eating disorders, and it often coexists with Binge Eating Disorder (BED). If psychiatric depression is a central factor or cause for binge eating, treating the condition may be more complicated. This raises the question of whether binge eating began because of depression or did depression begin because of binge eating.

Mental Health Issues:

Many people who have eating disorders also have mental health issues. The following are some examples of common experiences:

- depression
- anxiety

- obsessive-compulsive disorders
- phobias of certain food
- self-esteem and body image issues
- Self-harm in various forms – you may consider your eating disorder to be a form of self-harm, or you may harm yourself in other ways as well.
- Body dysmorphic disorder is an anxiety disorder that is related to one's appearance.

Anxiety, depression, and obsessive-compulsive behaviours can be conveyed in a variety of ways, including through food.

What impact could eating disorders have on my life?

- Food isn't the only problem with eating disorders. They may deal with difficult topics or painful emotions. These may be difficult for you to convey, face, or resolve.
- Even from yourself, focusing on food can be a way of hiding these emotions and problems. Eating disorders may have a variety of consequences.
- You may have the following thoughts:
- anxious and depressed
- a lot of the time I'm exhausted
- remorse or guilt
- I'm afraid of what other people would think if they find out.

You could come across:

- It's difficult to focus on your job, research, or hobbies.
- Food or eating control has become the most important aspect of your life.
- It's difficult to be spontaneous, travel, or visit somewhere new.
- Your physical appearance is undergoing or has undergone changes.
- You've been teased or bullied about your eating habits.
- you have short-term or long-term physical health issues
- You don't want to go out on dates, eat in restaurants, or eat in public.
- You may drop out of high school or college, leave your job, or give up activities that you enjoy.

When you're around mates, families, or other people, you might have the following feelings:

- You're cut off from people who don't understand or are frustrated that they can't do anything to assist.

- They emphasise the negative effects that eating disorders can have on your health.

- They only believe you have a problem if your body does not look the way they believe it should.
- They make tough comments about your appearance at times.
- They don't appreciate how difficult things are for you.

Losing your job to BED

People spend about half of your life at work. It's an important part of your social life, and it will help you increase (or deflate) your self-esteem. You must be alert, concentrated, energetic, and well rested in order to perform well at work.

You should expect recognition, opportunities, and promotions if you perform well. If you don't perform well, we all know what can happen.

So, how does a binge eating disorder (BED) affect your career? BEDs are a problem for a lot of people. According to studies, up to 2.6 percent of our adult population binge eats.

On a physical level

Binge eating puts the body under stress, making it work harder to digest, detoxify, and maintain balance. To make matters worse, many BED sufferers eat "comfort food" that is devoid of essential nutrients, such as ice cream, chips, sodas, and candy.

Not only does the body have to fight stronger to digest the food, wasting resources that could be used for work, but it still fails to obtain the necessary nutrients for mental distinctness. BEDs may have an impact on work performance over time.

On an emotional level

Binge eaters are more disturbed by anxiety and depression than similarly overweight people who do not binge.

BEDs can be vicious; they seem to relieve tension and fear, just to eventually expose itself as important factors to the same problems that the consumer believes they are exacerbating – depression and anxiety.

When you're stressed and nervous, your career fails. Your BED will put your job in jeopardy over time. And losing your job will exacerbate your anxiety and stress.

On a social level

Many BED sufferers gain weight over time. Their physical condition will deteriorate, and their energy levels will drop. They can eventually be easily annoyed and sensitive in response to comments, appearances, or neglected. Confidence will wane, leading to withdrawal or overcompensation for the BED's impacts. If this describes you, your friends and coworkers are noting that you aren't being "yourself."

The majority of workplaces prosper in a cooperative and friendly environment. You could eventually be more easily frustrated, distracted, or erratic as a result of your BED, impacting negatively on your job due to sluggish and unpredictable work results.

We don't always consider a BED to be something with professional ramifications. If you have a BED, seek therapy as soon as possible to reclaim your life before it has a negative impact on your physical health. It could mean the distinction between a job, financial support for your family, and self-esteem.

Anxiety and bed

Anxiety and binge eating disorder (BED) are closely linked and often co-occur.

In reality, about 37% of people with BED also have a full-fledged anxiety disorder. Anxiety and binge eating disorder are much more transactional than a linear relationship model would suggest (i.e., fear causes binge eating behaviours or binge eating behaviours causes anxiety). They are made up of biological, psychological, and social variables.

Factors in Biology

From a biological perspective, research teams are especially intrigued of the position of the neurochemical dopamine in the coexistence of BED and anxiety. Dopamine is implicated in rewarding and pleasurable sensations, particularly those related to food.

Dopamine

Binge eating, according to studies, releases dopamine, which relieves anxiety and depression. As a result, binge eating habits are reinforced. Some scholars compare this to a psychological reinforcement model used in substance abuse. Binge eaters, like people who use drugs to cope with negative emotions or mood states, have a similar problem.

Symptoms of Withdrawal

Binge eaters, including substance abusers, have withdrawal effects in between binge episodes, try to binge eat while thinking it's unhealthy, and feel deprived when they can't binge. These events are what cause BED symptoms, such as:

- Feeling out of control when it comes to your eating habits (i.e., the overeating feels unpreventable or unstoppable)
- Binging on at least three of the following foods:
- Quickly consuming food
- Consumption of food to the point of discomfort
- Not eating when you're not hungry
- Shame prevents me from eating with others.
- After overeating, I'm in a bad mood.
- Binge eating is a source of worry and concern.

Factors in Psychology

People with BED often feel panic, concern, or distress after bingeing, and negative feelings such as anxiety and depression often contribute to bingeing as a way to deal with these negative behaviours. Anxiety and binge feeding will quickly spiral into an out-of-control loop.

Changing a negative emotion for a more positive one

Researchers conclude that people with BED distract themselves from depressive thoughts by exchanging more aversive emotions they are having prior to binge-eating (e.g., sadness, anxiety) with fewer aversive emotions that occur after binge-eating (e.g., shame, guilt).

According to other studies, people with BED have high expectations about themselves, and when they don't achieve those expectations, they have a negative emotional reaction.

As a result, in order to escape these negative feelings, they pay more attention to their surroundings, which leads to a loss of appetite.

Factors of Society

Traumatic circumstances, such as a history of physical, sexual, or emotional abuse, as well as life stressors and interpersonal problems, can all increase the risk of BED and anxiety. Emotional eating can also be triggered by social pressures to be thin, which are also affected by the media.

People who are subjected to negative remarks about their bodies or weight (e.g., bullying, weight stigma) are more likely to have BED and anxiety.

Treatment for Bed and Anxiety Co-Occurrence

In terms of therapy, it's critical to address both binge eating and depressive mood states. When it comes to treating co-occurring BED and anxiety, cognitive-behavioral and interpersonal therapies appear to be the most effective.

In cognitive behavioural therapy, a mental-health professional assists a person with binge eating disorder in identifying, challenging, and reducing negative feelings and thought, as well as other dysfunctional belief systems that elicit unwanted behaviours.

The aim of interpersonal therapy is to identify and manage problems that a binge eating disorder sufferer may have in his or her interpersonal relationships.

When it comes to medications, selective serotonin reuptake inhibitors (SSRIs) prove to be the most effective therapy for co-occurring BED and anxiety. Some pharmacological therapies for BED that have been found to have some beneficial efficacy in patients with BED include tricyclic antidepressants, monoamine oxidase inhibitors, and opioid receptor antagonists.

Finding a team of professionals who will work closely to discuss the biological, psychological, and social complexities of co-occurring BED and anxiety is advantageous when receiving care.

Depression and BED

Many food-related disorders often co-occur with depression. It's not unusual to see a correlation between depression and binge eating disorder (BED).

Depression is described as a state of severe despondency and dejection that lasts for a long time and is followed by feelings of hopelessness and inadequacy.

BED is particularly popular in the United States, with one out of every ten people suffering from depression. BED is a disorder in which a person eats large amounts of food but does not purge.

BED is the most prevalent eating disorder in the United States today. Binge eating disorder affects 3.5 percent of women, 2% of men, and 30% to 40% of those seeking weight loss help.

Clinical Depression is a Life-Threatening Condition

Depression is often linked to a traumatic event, whether it occurred earlier in life or recently. Depression helps people feel as though they are holding a big weight on their shoulders at all times. It's not unusual for people to seek solace in their food. It's not only entertaining, but it's also a good way to pass the time.

When feeding, the person is not thinking about life's hopelessness or deep sorrow. Unfortunately, the behaviour does, and sometimes does, become addictive, resulting in severe medical and physical effects. This is because, unlike bulimia sufferers, BED sufferers should not purge. Obesity, along with all of its complications, is usually the result.

Depression and Eating Disorders: Is There a Link?

In the other hand, an eating disorder could be the starting point for a person. This, too, is often attributed to trauma. A young girl may suffer from an apparently minor but ongoing trauma like bullying, or a woman may suffer from a major traumatic event like rape.

In any case, they may be plagued by painful memories and feelings related to the trauma.

She, like those who suffer from depression, tries to cope with her emotions by eating. When someone gains weight, the mental pain begins, and her life narrows as food becomes her closest friend, depression is normal.

It Is Possible To recover

Thankfully, complete recovery is possible regardless of how these co-occurring illnesses manifest themselves in a person's life. Due to the nature of the two conditions arising at the same time, residential or inpatient care may be required; but, at the end of the day, an individual may feel depression relief and a healthier interaction with food.

Adolescents Depression and BED

Many adolescents with binge eating disorders, which are marked by the uncontrollable consumption of huge amounts of food particularly though they are not emotionally starving, are often at risk for depression. The opposite is also correct: people who are stressed are more likely to begin binge eating.

While it's unknown that the two frequently coexist, study has found that many individuals live in isolation when either or more diseases go undiagnosed and untreated.

Consider it this way: You're depressed because you ate too much, or you're depressed because you ate too much. For binge eaters, this vicious spiral is unstoppable, leaving feelings of remorse and humiliation, as well as other unpleasant emotions generally associated with depression, for-example:

- Interest in activities has waned
- Extreme sorrow and/or dissatisfaction
- Sleeping problems
- Irritableness
- despondency
- Suicidal ideation

To make matters worse, binge eating can lead to weight gain, which can be a cause of additional stress for teens who are continually comparing themselves to their peers and who are vulnerable to social rejection, loneliness, and bullying for any attribute seen as different or unwelcome.

Individualizing a Plan to Meet Individual Needs

Adolescent parents are often at a loss about how to intervene. Some parents may chastise or reprimand their child for overeating and weight gain, further aggravating the problem.

The good news is that recovery from binge eating disorders with underlying depression is possible, and it requires a plan that is tailored to each person's needs and addresses both conditions at the same time.

Intensive Outpatient Programs (IOPs)

Intensive Outpatient Programs (IOPs) are a type of outpatient treatment that Formal programmes, such as partial hospitals or intensive outpatient programmes, often provide pre-assembled teams of experts who collaborate to create an adequate treatment plan that addresses all of an adolescent's binge-eating disorder's needs.

Typically, these programmes include specialised therapy aimed at providing emotional support and repairing damaged self-esteem. Antidepressant medication may be necessary to lift the cloud of depression that causes the adolescent to believe he or she is helpless.

Parental Guidance

In their child's therapy and rehab, parents play a critical part. This could include eating more regularly, altering routines to provide guidance, and including their child in more physical activity.

Inpatient or hospitalisation programmes are available.

A hospital or residential programme may be the best or only option in situations where the problem has advanced beyond the scope of outpatient care. Binge-related depression may progress to the point where the child is no longer safe at home due to suicidal thoughts or self-harming behaviour.

Furthermore, conditions such as uncontrolled diabetes, frequent asthma attacks, and/or extreme high blood pressure may make binge-related weight gain medically dangerous.

Consider These Factors When Choosing a Treatment

There are professional resources available, but what you can get depends on where you live and what kind of health insurance you have. Factors to consider when choosing a programme include:

- what distance is it from your home and the care facility?
- What is your impression of the programme? Are you being helpful? Is it responsive?
- What services are available and who delivers them?
- What does the treatment plan entail?
- Is your insurance approved in that location?

Remember that having a binge eating disorder or depression, whether you or someone close to you is affected, is not a sign of weakness. It's also not something that can be overcome solely through the application of willpower. Many people live with these conditions on a daily basis and need assistance to improve.

The Initial Steps Toward Recovery

The first move is to admit that there is a problem. An observant, caring, and persistent parent will be expected to transcend the teenager's innate unwillingness and guilt to accept there is an issue and continue the recovery process for the adolescent and their families.

The right treatment will help you restore your trust as well as your physical and mental health. Getting help has helped a lot of people, and it will help you or a loved one as well.

Mindfulness/DBT and BED

Binge eating cravings can strike without warning and leave the sufferer in a state of disarray, confusion, guilt, and fear.

Binge eating disorder recovery also entails a combination of strategies and psychotherapy to help a person reclaim their life and freedom from binge eating.

Because of the complexities of binge eating disorder, therapy must be thorough and include a variety of evidence-based approaches in order to achieve the best results. When a person's treatment progresses, they can also learn how to better manage bingeing impulses.

Other options for Traditional Recovery Techniques

Mindfulness and Dialectical Behavior Therapy are two traditional approaches to binge eating disorder treatment that are sometimes learned (DBT). While some people may be sceptical of these psychotherapy techniques at first, many people will find that they are effective in dealing with binge eating urges that can occur at any point during their recovery from binge eating disorder.

People with binge eating disorder have been shown to benefit from DBT and other psychotherapy interventions. What are the methods and procedures that will aid in the recovery of someone suffering from Binge Eating Disorder?

How Does Mindfulness Work?

Mindfulness entails being aware of what we are thinking, feeling, and experiencing in the present moment, including what we are thinking, feeling, and the environment in which we are immersed.

There's more to mindfulness than that. It's also the practise of acknowledging whatever thoughts and feelings we're having rather than passing judgement on what's going on right now.

Although mindfulness began as a Buddhist meditation practise in the east, its introduction into western practises has proved useful to countless people suffering from a range of ailments.

Mindfulness Practices Have Many Advantages

What are the benefits of using mindfulness-based treatments to help with binge eating recovery? The following are some of the ways that mindfulness techniques can be beneficial:

- Eating With Intention

Mindful eating can help a person become more aware of their

thoughts, emotions, feelings, and behaviours. Although eating disorders can essentially dull feelings, practising mindfulness before a binge can help a person think on how they are feeling.

This can lead to questions like, "Am I really hungry, or do I need something else right now?" and "How am I feeling?" Reflecting on such questions can help someone work through binge eating urges and figure out what they really need to stay healthy.

- Stress and Anxiety Reduction

Many binge eaters use food as a coping mechanism for stress and anxiety. By helping a person to process rather than hide behind their thoughts, mindfulness-based practises may be therapeutic in learning how to better cope with outside stressors that could be triggering binge feeding.

- Making Peace with Your Body and Food

When a person learns to embrace themselves in the current moment, mindfulness-based therapy interventions will help them come to terms with their feelings and bodies. This will happen gradually as a person begins to accept and experience current emotions without criticising them.

DBT and How it Works

DBT is a form of psychotherapy that has been used to aid in the recovery of individuals suffering from Binge Eating Disorder. DBT emphasises the practise of mindfulness and other relaxation methods.

DBT is helpful for those with mental dysregulation, such as binge eating disorder, and it shows patients how to embrace rather than avoid negative emotions or emotions. Mindfulness is incorporated into DBT counselling to show people how to perceive their feelings thoroughly and without judgement, as well as how to view their surroundings with perspective.

When used as part of a holistic recovery strategy, DBT will help reduce the occurrence of bingeing episodes while simultaneously teaching healthier coping skills.

DBT should also be carried out under the supervision of a competent and experienced therapist, preferably one who specialises in eating disorder recovery. To help patients recover from binge eating habits, medication counselling, prescription diet treatment, and other types of psychotherapy, such as CBT and interpersonal therapy, can be used in combination with DBT (IPT).

Tools for Long-Term Recovery that are Priceless

Binge eating disorder, for example, effectively numbs a woman's or man's desires while simultaneously isolating them from their surroundings and environment. Although binge eating disorder may help certain people "cope" with difficult conditions, it may also be crippling.

Mindfulness and DBT can be particularly helpful in the detox process when used as part of a systematic, evidence-based therapy for binge eating disorder.

If you or someone you care for is recovering from binge eating disorder, it's important to get health treatment, counselling, and guidance. You don't have to go through this alone, because there are plenty of options to help you overcome binge eating disorder. Making touch with an eating disorder specialist will help you figure out the best recovery option for you.

Children's Binge Eating and the Rise in Childhood Obesity in the United States

Across the country, health professionals, politicians, and others have raised concerns about children's binge eating and obesity. 1/3 of children and young people were overweight or obese in 2012. In the last thirty years, childhood obesity has more than multiplied by 2 in children and multiplied by 4 in teens.

Families may be confused about how to handle their growing children as a result of the reaction to this epidemic, which has sent several mixed messages. Could a country obsessed with childhood obesity, combined with a culture saturated with disillusioned media, be leading to an increase in eating disorders among younger generations?

Obesity Increasing, and Binge Eating in Children?

Obesity among adolescents and teens in the United States has risen, but so has the number of children who binge eat. Many well-intentioned parents and guardians can want to place their child or teenager on a diet because they are unsure how to cope with the common misinformation regarding childhood obesity. The fear of being obese can lead to a variety of negative changes in an effort to lose weight.

This may entail:

- Restricting high-fat, high-sugar, and high-carbohydrate diets
- Keeping portion proportions in check
- Eliminating a whole food category
- Excessive activity and exercise
- Allowing a child to avoid eating "fun foods" or participating in activities where certain foods are available

While these ideas may have good intentions, dieting as a child may set the stage for a serious eating disorder, such as BED. Dieting is not only ineffective in children and adolescents, but it can also lead to poor eating habits, weight gain, and/or obesity.

Girls and women who have dieted account for approximately two-thirds of new cases of eating disorders.

Unhealthy Food Relationships Can Be Caused by Childhood Diets

Children who are exposed to dieting behaviours develop a disdain for their bodies and their natural intuitive food instincts. As a result of a fear of such foods being "evil" or a general mistrust of their bodies, many children form an unhealthy association with food, which can lead to binge feeding in infants.

In some cases, making a certain food or food group "forbidden," either by limiting or banning it, may actually make that food more appealing to a child. When it comes to eating and food choices, these kinds of habits can create a sense of chaos and "lack of control."

This can lead to erratic dietary patterns and behaviours, such as missing meals, hoarding food, and overeating, among other things.

If a child has binge eating disorder, they may show specific signs and symptoms, which may include:

- Binge eating, or eating a lot of meals in a short period of time, on a regular basis
- When you're bingeing, you'll eat a lot of food quickly.
- Continuing to eat after you've reached your limit
- Feelings of humiliation or embarrassment cause you to eat alone.
- Consumption of food to the point of physical discomfort
- After binge eating, you may feel guilty, disgusted, or ashamed.

Eating disorders, such as binge eating disorder, are caused

by a number of causes, including biology, atmosphere, which psychology, and may have drastic repercussions.

Environmental causes, such as chronic dieting exposure, may be particularly triggering for an infant who already has certain risk factors for binge eating disorder, such as a genetic predisposition or a family history of the disorder.

This is especially worrying for infants, who are young and at a crucial developmental stage.

It's also worth mentioning that parents aren't to blame for their child's eating disorder, and that understanding eating disorder behaviours will actually help parents embrace early diagnosis and recovery.

Encouraging Good Eating Habits and a Positive Body Image

Encourage children to have a healthy respect and appreciation for their bodies, and they will want to take good care of them. Remind children of the amazing systems that are constantly at work in their bodies to keep them alive.

The beauty of a strong heart pumping blood across their bodies, healthy lungs that they breathe, and strong legs that take them to the playground. These kinds of remarks allow kids to think of their bodies as highly functional and to want to take good care of them.

There's a lot of pressure to prioritise weight loss over overall wellness.

Many parents may be under scrutiny from the outside world; whether it's from the public, health providers, peers, or relatives, parents may be second-guessing how they're parenting their children, eating habits, or whether they're at a healthier weight.

While determining which practises are better for your family's wellbeing can be challenging, remember to foster and promote your child's innate connection with food and their bodies.

Children who are not hindered by external factors are able to instinctively self-regulate their diet and decide how much and what foods to consume in a given day.

You can empower your child as a parent by:

- Modeling a positive attitude toward food and your body
- Meals with the family
- Taking the emphasis off of weight loss and dieting

Keeping an Eye Out for Warning Signs

It's also crucial to recognise the early warning signs of eating disorders. Although admitting that your child has an eating disorder can be overwhelming, being mindful of the condition can lead to early diagnosis and recovery.

Children with binge eating disorder will benefit from a structured recovery plan that includes the help of a family doctor, nurse, nutritionist, and counsellor.

If you're concerned with your child's eating patterns or weight, seek the advice of a qualified health provider who will assist you with caring for your loved one.

If your child is showing the onset of binge eating disorder, a licenced eating disorder specialist should decide if professional action is required. An eating disorder's prognosis and conditions can be improved if it is detected and treated early.

And if things feel daunting, keep in mind that you are not alone, and there are many tools available to help you along your parenting path.

12

Helplines And Statistics

Going to a support group seeking assistance with an eating disorder would be very helpful. You'd be able to chat with those who are experiencing similar problems. This will assist you in realizing that you are not alone in the fight against an eating disorder. Millions of people all over the world are dealing with similar issues, and they all have the same pessimistic feelings as you.

Being able to actively engage with people who suffer from eating disorders would allow you to support one another. By doing well, you will feel confident in helping to inspire others. You'll be able to reach out to the community for support on days when you're feeling especially bad. You will become united as a group and begin to resolve eating disorder problems.

There are several eating disorder support groups to choose from. Some of these types would concentrate on a single eating disorder. For example, there might be a programme dedicated to assisting individuals suffering from anorexia. Another category would concentrate on people who struggle with binge eating.

It could be as easy as conducting a Google search to locate the best group to assist you. You'll be able to communicate with those who are living through or have lived through severe difficulties. And if you think you've conquered your eating problem, it's always a good idea to hang around to support others. Others will be inspired by your performance to properly treat their condition.

Helplines:

United States

National Crisis Line - Anorexia and Bulimia: 1-800-233-4357

United Kingdom

B-eat (Beat Eating Disorders)
   Helpline: 0808 801 0677

(Make sure you look for your countries best websites and resources on the internet and the one that suits you the best)

Anyone suffering from an eating disorder, such as anorexia or bulimia nervosa, can get advice, help, and updates from good resources that are online. You just need to do good research on the one that is best for you.

There are some of them:

Bolster is a telephone coaching service for sufferers that aims to boost their confidence as they heal.

Nexus is a telephone coaching and advice programme for caregivers who are helping a loved one.

Solace is a video community for caregivers led by professional eating disorder clinicians that is peer-supported.

Raising Resilience is a new workshop for someone who cares for someone who has an eating disorder and wants to learn how to help their loved one get better.

National Centre for Eating Disorders

Helpline: 0845 838 2040

Supporting your child with eating problems

Both children and young people's mental health is a priority for this national charity. The Parents' Information Service, for example, is a free, anonymous helpline for any adult with questions regarding a child or young person's mental health.

Family Lives

Helpline: 0808 800 2222 (24 hours)

Facts and Statistics

The following is a list of binge eating disorder facts and statistics:

- In the United States, BED is the most prevalent eating disorder.
- BED affects people of all ages, races, and demographics.
- 3.5 percent of adult women and 2% of adult men suffer from BED.
- Women account for about 60% of BED sufferers.
- BED affects 2.3 percent of female adolescents and 0.8 percent of male adolescents.
- BED usually begins between the ages of 18 and 29 for women.
- BED usually begins in men between the ages of 45 and 59.
- BED in adults is described as at least one binge per week for three months.

- BED is described as at least one binge per month for three months in children or adolescents.
- Overweight or obese people make up a large proportion of BED sufferers.

13

Review page

As an independent author with a small marketing budget, reviews are my likelihood on this platform. If you enjoyed this book, I'd really appreciate it if you'd left your honest feedback. You can do so by clicking the link below. I love hearing from my readers and I personally read every single review.

PLEASE LEAVE A REVIEW:

14

Conclusion

Conclusion

O kay, friends, these are the steps you need to take to avoid binge eating, as well as all the details you'll need. Have you realised how easy it is yet? This stuff works, what you have to do now is put it into practice.

15

Resources Page

R esources page

- *Eating problems.* (2017, June). Mind for Better Mental Health. https://www.devonmind.com/info-resources/mental-health-problems/eating-problems
- Kumari, S. K. (2020, October 10). *All You Need To Know About Binge Eating Disorder: Does It Need A Treatment?* Healthwire. https://www.healthwire.co/all-you-need-to-know-about-binge-eating-disorder-does-it-need-a-treatment/
- Mandl, E. M. (2019, December 3). *Binge Eating Disorder: Symptoms, Causes, and Asking for Help.* Healthline. https://www.healthline.com/nutrition/binge-eating-disorder
- *Overeating: Symptoms, Causes, and Seeking help.* (n.d.). The Wellness Checks. Retrieved March 25, 2021, from https://thewellnesschecks.com/food-

beverages/overeating-symptoms-causes-and-see king-help/#respond

- Schaeffer, J. S. (2016, December 18). *What's the Difference Between Overeating and Binge Eating Disorder?* Healthline. https://www.healthline.co m/health/eating-disorders/compulsive-overeati ng-vs-binge-eating-disorder
- Smith, M. S., Robinson, L. R., & Segal, J. S. (n.d.). *Binge Eating Disorder.* HelpGuide. Retrieved March 23, 2021, from https://www.helpguide. org/articles/eating-disorders/binge-eating-disor der.htm

Made in the USA
Coppell, TX
23 April 2023

15947554R10095